A Key to the Genera of
GRASSES
of the Conterminous
United States
[6th edition]

by
James Payne Smith, Jr.
Professor of Botany
Director of the Herbarium
Humboldt State University
Arcata, California

August 1981

MAD RIVER PRESS INC.

© James Payne Smith, Jr.

ISBN 0-916422-22-4

Published by   Mad River Press, Inc.
                Route 2, Box 151-B
                Eureka, California 95501

Printed by   Eureka Printing Company
                106 T Street
                Eureka, California 95501

stolon provides a means of vegetative reproduction for the grass.

The grass leaf is differentiated into **blade**, **sheath**, and **ligule**. The blade is typically strap- or ribbon-shaped, with parallel veins of vascular tissue running its length. The lower portion of the leaf is the sheath, a tubular collar that surrounds the culm. Some morphologists interpret it as a flattened petiole. In most instances, the two edges of the sheath touch one another or overlap. but are not organically fused. In this case the sheath is said to be **open**. In some grasses, including the commonly encountered bromes, the two edges are fused with one another to form a continuous cylinder, thereby creating a **closed** sheath. You will discover that it is not as easy to determine this feature as these definitions suggest. The mechanical action of the wind can tear the upper section of a closed sheath, making it appear open. Look closely at several sheaths before committing yourself. You will find that many grasses have a membranous flap, series of hairs, or a combination of both structures on the upper surface of the blade at the point where it joins the sheath. This feature is the **ligule**. Its size and shape are of diagnostic value. Some grasses, especially those of the barley tribe, also have small, paired, ear-like flaps at the top of the sheath. These are **auricles**.

Flowers

Culms may remain vegetative or produce flowers. Most of us have never seen these tiny structures and we may not even be aware that grasses are flowering plants. The reasons are understandable. Grass flowers are small and hidden away from easy view by a system of **bracts** or reduced leaves. The brightly-colored sepals and petals that make the somewhat distantly related lilies and orchids so attractive were eventually lost through the gradual processes of evolutionary reduction. All that remains of these floral envelopes are microscopic flaps called **lodicules**. Luckily, we will not be using many characters derived from grass flowers in this key.

The reproductive components of the flower have been retained and modified for wind pollination. The **androecium**, or male part of the flower, is made up of **stamens**. Each one consists of a delicate, thread-like supporting stalk called a **filament** and a terminal sac-like region of pollen-producing tissue, the **anther**. Most grasses have three stamens, some have two or one, and a few have six. The **gynoecium**, or female part of the flower, consists of a seed-producing structure, the **ovary**, and a terminal pair of feathery **stigmas** that trap airborne pollen. The ovary will form a single-seeded fruit, the **grain** or **caryopsis**, at maturity.

Grass flowers vary in the presence or absence of reproductive parts. A **perfect** flower is one that has both an androecium and a gynoecium. A **pistillate** flower has only the seed-producing component, the gynoecium; while a **staminate** one has only the complement of stamens. A **neuter** or

sterile flower lacks both types of reproductive organs. Once again, what is easily defined on paper becomes difficult to interpret under the hand lens or dissecting microscope. All grass keys will require the user to distinguish between perfect, staminate, pistillate, or neuter conditions. Look at several flowers before deciding. One of the more common causes of misinterpretation arises when anthers develop early, shed their pollen, shrivel, and fall from the plant. A quick glance will lead to the mistaken notion that the flower is pistillate. Look carefully for filaments as a clue to the presence of fallen stamens.

Spikelet Structure

Because of their small size, high degree of evolutionary reduction, and lack of easily observed features, grass flowers have not been used as the basis for distinguishing genera and species. Instead, the classification has been based upon the structure of bracts that enclose individual grass flowers and that subtend clusters of them.

Grass flowers, the minute stalks that support them, and the bract system associated with them make up a unit called a **spikelet**. Some of them, especially those containing a single flower, may be quite small. Others, notably those with several to many flowers, may be a few centimeters long and easily seen without magnification. The spikelet, although characteristic of the grass family, is not its exclusive property. Plants of the sedge family have them, too. Because their spikelets are of superficially the same construction, it is easy to confuse the two families. More about this later.

All grass spikelets are put together in the same basic fashion (see plate 2). The tiny flowers and bracts are attached directly or indirectly to an unbranched central axis or internal stalk, the **rachilla**. At the base of the rachilla are two bracts that are empty or sterile, in that they do not have flowers inserted directly above them. Each of these two basal bracts of the spikelet is a **glume**. It is traditional to refer to the one that is inserted slightly below the other on the rachilla as the **first glume**; its partner is the **second glume**. The two glumes may be similar in length, width, and shape or noticeably different from one another. They may also vary in the number of **nerves**, the strands of vascular tissue running their length.

In addition to the pair of glumes, a spikelet is made up of one or more **florets**, each inserted at its own node on the rachilla. A floret consists of a single flower and two bracts, the **lemma** and **palea**, that enclose it. It is important to note that a floret never has more than one flower and that the terms floret and flower are not synonymous. The number of florets per spikelet is of great diagnostic significance. A spikelet with a single floret is called **one-flowered**; one with two florets is said to be **two-flowered**, and so on.

The lemma and palea are the source of many taxonomic features. The

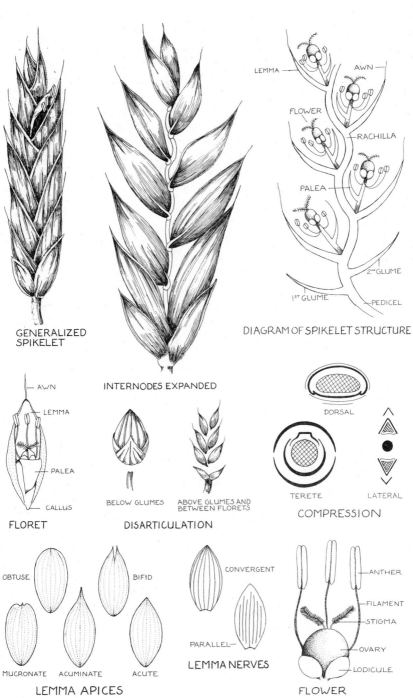

GENERALIZED
SPIKELET

INTERNODES EXPANDED

DIAGRAM OF SPIKELET STRUCTURE

LEMMA

FLOWER

PALEA

AWN

RACHILLA

2ⁿᵈ GLUME

1ˢᵀ GLUME

PEDICEL

AWN

LEMMA

PALEA

CALLUS

FLORET

BELOW GLUMES

ABOVE GLUMES AND
BETWEEN FLORETS

DISARTICULATION

DORSAL

TERETE

LATERAL

COMPRESSION

OBTUSE

BIFID

MUCRONATE   ACUMINATE   ACUTE

LEMMA APICES

CONVERGENT

PARALLEL

LEMMA NERVES

ANTHER

FILAMENT

STIGMA

OVARY

LODICULE

FLOWER

PLATE 2. SPIKELET STRUCTURE.

lemma is typically the larger and firmer of the two bracts, its edges often partially obscuring the palea. The lemma typically has an odd number of nerves, with one, three, five, seven, and nine being very common. Occasionally it will appear nerveless. Counting nerve number can be challenging. It is very easy to overlook submarginal nerves, those that lie close to the edge of the bract. In most instances the nerves of the lemma will converge with one another toward the apex, but in a few grasses they remain parallel to one another.

The lemma will often appear as a rounded bract when viewed in cross-section. Sometimes it is conspicuously folded or V-shaped. It may also have a prominent rib or **keel** running down its center, a term derived from the structure on the bottom of a boat.

The apex of a glume or lemma may bear a short, sharp point. This is a **mucro** and the bract that bears this structure is **mucronate**. These same bracts may also bear a more elongate, substantial, hair-like projection called an **awn**. It may be from a few millimeters to several centimeters in length. Awns may be straight, bent, or twisted. While lemmas are commonly awned, it is most unusual for the palea to bear this feature. An awn need not be terminal. Some are inserted on the back of a bract at about its midpoint, while in other species the awn arises at or near the base. Awns are the source of several features used in this key.

The hardened base of a lemma or floret is the **callus**. In some instances, the callus is made up of lemma and rachilla tissue. It may be rounded or even sharp-pointed, as in the needle grasses. The callus may be without hairs to almost totally obscured by a conspicuous beard.

Unlike the lemma, the palea is not the source of many taxonomic features. It tends to be a delicate, membranous, 2-nerved, awnless bract. The palea may be as long as the lemma, but it is often slightly shorter.

Spikelets are either round (**terete**) or flattened (**compressed**) when viewed in cross-section. Terete spikelets are relatively uncommon, but they do occur in such genera as *Stipa*, the needle grasses. Compressed spikelets are of two types. If the bracts are flattened from the sides, the spikelet is **laterally compressed**; if flattened as though pressure were brought to bear from the backs of the bracts, then **dorsally compressed**.

At maturity, spikelets will break apart at predetermined points of separation. This process is called **disarticulation**. In many grasses, disarticulation occurs just below the first glume, so that the entire spikelet falls from the plant, leaving only a bare stalk. In many other grasses, disarticulation occurs above the glume and between the florets. They fall separately or in clusters, sometimes with prominent segments of the rachilla remaining attached. There is a tendency for spikelets with lateral compression to disarticulate above the glume, while those of dorsal compression disarticulate below the glumes. There are many exceptions to this generality.

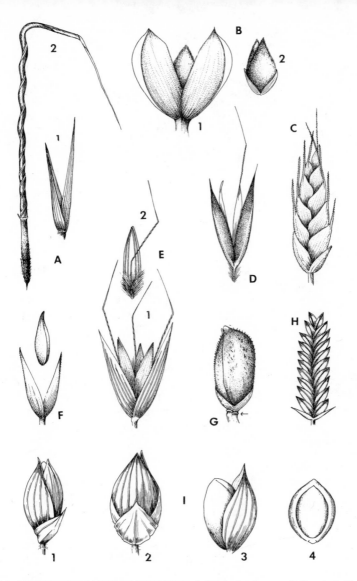

PLATE 3. VARIATION IN SPIKELET TYPES. A. *Stipa*. 1, glumes; 2, floret. B. *Phalaris*. 1, spikelet; 2, fertile floret and two highly reduced, subtending florets. C. *Bromus* spikelet with its several fertile florets. The lemmas are several-nerved. D. *Andropogon* spikelet with its relatively firm glumes; a delicate, awned floret; and a membranous, sterile lemma. E. *Avena*. 1, spikelet with three, awned florets; 2, isolated floret. F. *Agrostis* spikelet with single floret isolated from the glumes. G. *Oryza* spikelet with single fertile floret; reduced, sterile lemmas; and rudimentary glumes (indicated by arrow). H. *Eragrostis* spikelet with its numerous florets. The lemmas are three-nerved. !. *Panicum* spikelet. 1, side view showing small first glume (right), larger second glume (left), and sterile lemma (right); 2, front view showing small first glume, partially enveloping edges of the second glume, and sterile lemma; 3, sterile lemma (right) and fertile floret (left); 4, fertile floret.

To summarize, then, a typical grass spikelet consists of two glumes and one or more florets inserted on a rachilla. It is laterally or dorsally compressed, or less often terete. The spikelet disarticulates above or below the glumes. The glumes and/or the lemmas may be awned. While this is the basic theme, it is subject to a whole series of modifications. One of the most important of these is reduction and loss of spikelet parts. One or both glumes may be missing. In spikelets with more than one floret, the upper ones are often smaller than the lower ones and they may be sterile. Sometimes the uppermost floret is well-developed, and fertile, while the one or two florets subtending it are reduced. In a few instances, the middle florets are well-developed, while those above and below are sterile. In these reduced florets, the lemma is referred to as a **sterile lemma** because it lacks the flower in its axil that is typical of the fertile lemma. In a few grasses, such as the bent grasses of the genus *Agrostis,* the palea may be quite small or even absent. This variation can be troublesome for the beginning student, but proper interpretation can be more easily assured if you take the time to learn the basic positional relationships of spikelet parts.

Because there is only one flower per floret, we can carry over the terminology developed earlier for describing reproductive completeness. If a flower is perfect, then the floret of which it is a part is also termed perfect. A **staminate floret** is, then, a floret which contains a staminate flower. One curious bit of tradition is that a floret that bears a functional ovary is said to be a **fertile floret**, regardless of the presence or absence of stamens.

Inflorescences

Culms, whether they be primary stems, side branches, or stolons, often emerge from their sheaths and bear one to several hundred spikelets. This flowering portion of the grass plant is its **inflorescence**. A culm may bear one or more of them. If the spikelet cluster emerges from the uppermost sheath, it is a **terminal inflorescence**. If it arises from a lower sheath on that same culm, it is **axillary** or **lateral**. It is sometimes difficult for the beginning student to determine how much of what he or she sees constitutes a single inflorescence. A simple rule is that there are never any well-developed foliage leaves within an inflorescence. Whether terminal or axillary, the uppermost spikelet and the first foliage leaf mark the top and base of an individual inflorescence.

The upper portion of the culm that supports the entire inflorescence is the **peduncle**, while the stalk that supports an individual spikelet is the **pedicel**. If there is a clearly defined central axis within the inflorescence, it is called a **rachis**. Note that this term applies to the axis of the entire inflorescence, while rachilla is the central stalk within a spikelet. The rachis is sometimes enlarged and thickened, with spikelets partially embedded in its tissues.

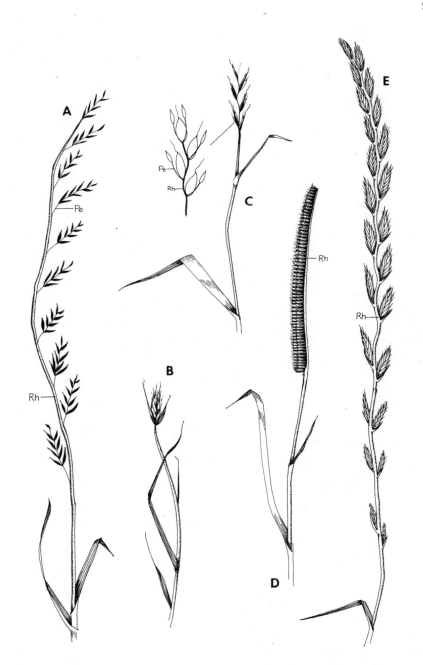

PLATE 4. INFLORESCENCE TYPES. A. Simple raceme of *Pleuropogon*. B. Solitary spikelet of *Danthonia*. C. Simple rame of *Schizachyrium*. D. Simple, one-sided spike of *Ctenium*. E. Simple, balanced spike of *Lolium*. In all drawings. Pe = pedicel and Rh = rachis.

The exact arrangement of spikelets determines the inflorescence type. You will find this terminology frustrating because various authors use these words in different ways. The scheme used in this key is as follows:

1) **spike**—a very common inflorescence type in which the spikelets are inserted directly on an unbranched rachis. Pedicels are, for all practical purposes, lacking. The number of spikelets inserted at any given node along the rachis varies with the kind of grass.

2) **raceme**—an inflorescence in which spikelets are borne on well-developed pedicels arising from an unbranched rachis. Typically the spikelets are in pairs or trios at a node, their pedicels of equal or unequal length. Infrequently, there may be a single spikelet at a node, as in the semaphore grasses. The distinction between the spike and raceme is based upon degree of development of the pedicel. While that difference is entirely arbitrary, I have attempted to say that any spikelet with a pedicel more than about 1 mm in length is pedicellate.

3) **rame**—a specialized modification of the raceme, more or less restricted to the barley and bluestem tribes, in which pedicellate and sessile spikelets occur together in pairs or trios. The pedicels may be of equal or unequal length.

4) **panicle**—in this most common of inflorescence types, the rachis bears primary and secondary branches, ending in pedicels that bear the spikelets. In other words, the inflorescence is much-branched and spikelets are not inserted directly on the rachis as they are in the spike, raceme, or rame. A panicle may be open and diffuse or contracted, dense, and closed.

5) **solitary spikelet**—an unusual, reduced inflorescence. as in poverty oats, in which the peduncle bears a single spikelet. This inflorescence type is thought to be a result of evolutionary reduction of some other type, especially the panicle.

6) **compound spike**—an inflorescence in which the peduncle bears two or more branches, each a spike of spikelets.

7) **compound raceme**—an inflorescence in which the peduncle bears two or more branches, each a raceme of spikelets.

8) **compound rame**—an inflorescence in which the peduncle bears two or more branches, each a rame of spikelets.

In the spike, raceme, or rame the spikelets may be more or less evenly inserted on opposite sides of the rachis so that the inflorescence is **balanced**, or obviously situated with the majority of spikelets on one side of the rachis, so that it is **one-sided**.

In compound inflorescences, the branches may be distributed along the rachis (**racemose**), or they may be clustered at the apex of the peduncle, radiating as do fingers on the hand (**digitate**).

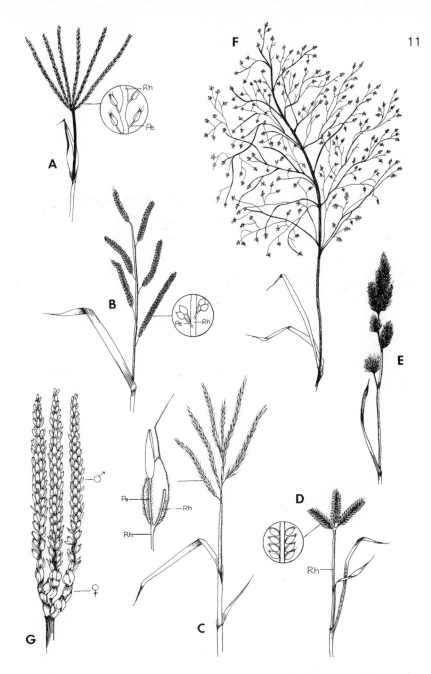

PLATE 5. INFLORESCENCE TYPES. A. Compound, digitate raceme of *Digitaria*. B. Compound, racemose racemes of *Paspalum*. C. Compound rames of *Andropogon*. D. Compound, digitate spikes of *Dactyloctenium*. E. Condensed panicle of *Muhlenbergia*. F. Open panicle of *Eragrostis*. G. Mixed inflorescence of *Tripsacum* with its distinctive pistillate and staminate spikelets. In all drawings, Pe = pedicel and Rh = rachis.

BOTANICAL AND GEOGRAPHICAL SCOPE OF THE KEY

It is the purpose of this key to provide a means for the identification of the genus for all native, introduced, and adventive grasses in the United States. Only those grasses that are strictly cultivated as ornamentals, crop plants, or experimental subjects are omitted. One new feature of this edition is a list of excluded genera, together with a brief explanation as to why these do not appear in the keys.

The phrase "conterminous United States" merely indicates that the geographic limit is the 48 states that are adjacent to one another; Alaska and Hawaii are excluded.

HOW TO USE THE KEY

The first step in using this key is to make certain that the plant you wish to identify is a grass. As I mentioned earlier, it is relatively easy to confuse them with sedges. The following table summarizes a series of features that will serve to distinguish plants of the two families.

Feature	Grasses	Sedges
Stem:		
Cross-section	round [flat] [a]	triangular [round] [a]
Internodes	hollow [solid]	solid
Leaves:		
Ranks [b]	two	three
Sheaths	open [closed]	closed
Ligule	present	absent
Spikelets:		
Bracts	distichous [c]	distichous or spiral
Bracts/flowers	2 (lemma and palea)	1 (glume or scale)
Flowers:		
Perianth	two [three] lodicules	6-0 bristles
Stamen number	3 [2 or 1]	1-3
Anther attachment	"versatile"	basifixed
Stigma number	two	two or three
Carpel number	two	two or three
Fruit:		
Type	caryopsis	achene
Embryo position	lateral	central

a=unusual condition stated inside brackets
b=number of vertical rows. expressed as two-ranked, three-ranked, etc.
c=inserted in two vertical rows. 2-ranked

Now that you have determined that the unknown plant is a grass, the next step is to place it in one of eight "Groups", using the "Key to Groups" on page 16. If you are unfamiliar with keys, a brief explanation is in order. A key is a logical device for the identification of unknown organisms. It consists of a series of paired, parallel, and contrasting statements describing one or more features of the plant or animal. The numbered statements are paired to form a couplet, in that there are only two of them at each step in the key. They are parallel because they address the same feature of the known; contrasting because the two halves of the couplet are mutually exclusive—the unknown can fit under only one of the two choices. Each statement in a key will lead to the name of an organism or to a number directing you to a subsequent couplet in the series.

Inflorescence types are an important feature in this key. I assume that you will observe them at arm's length; no close examination is encouraged in the preliminary key to groups. I have not distinguished between the true spike and those racemes, rames, and condensed panicles that are spike-like. You will have to be more critical in later sections of the key, however.

Once the unknown grass has been placed in the proper Group, turn to that section of the key and proceed with the determination of the genus. Eighty of the 190 genera of U.S. grasses are represented in this country by a single species. In these instances, I have supplied you with the complete scientific name. Otherwise, it will be necessary to consult a flora or some other reference if you wish to go beyond genus. The *Manual of the Grasses of the United States* by A.S. Hitchcock, as revised by Agnes Chase, remains the single most useful work on the grasses of this country. The page number in Hitchcock and Chase where descriptions, illustrations, and species keys can be found is provided for each genus. A series of numbered notes, appearing as superscripts, gives changes in generic and scientific names, as well as commentary on taxonomic concepts. A list of literature useful for the identification of U.S. grasses appears on page 66.

ACKNOWLEDGMENTS

It is a pleasure to thank Joseph DiTomaso, Jennifer Whipple Hutchinson, Teresa Prendusi, and the students in my Agrostology classes at Humboldt State University. Their suggestions and corrections have been very helpful in the preparation of this edition. I am also grateful to Frank Gould of Texas A&M University, Richard Pohl of Iowa State University, John Reeder of Arizona State University, Thomas Soderstrom of the Smithsonian Institution, and G. Ledyard Stebbins of the University of California at Davis for their kind assistance in evaluating generic concepts. Special thanks go to Linda Sharakan, whose illustrations appear on the cover and in the introductory section. Her work adds much to the usefulness of this edition.

Arcata on the Mad

JPS
August 1981

KEY TO GROUPS

1. Robust perennials, typically two to several meters tall, bamboo-like or with large, plume-like inflorescences; culms woody to very tough and inflexible, one to several centimeters in diameter ....
.... **Group A** (p. 18)

1. Annuals to perennials, typically less than 1.5 m tall, not at all bamboo-like, nor with large, plume-like inflorescences; culms strictly herbaceous, less than 0.5 cm in diameter **2**

    2. Inflorescence (or inflorescences in the case of some unisexual grasses) of spikelets of two distinct and obviously different forms, these differences clearly visible without magnification
.... **Group B** (p. 20)

    2. Inflorescence of spikelets of the same form, varying perhaps in minor details of construction, but these differences not easily seen without dissection and magnification **3**

3. Inflorescence a single spike, raceme, rame, spike-like panicle, or head-like clump of spikelets; no inflorescence branches easily seen at arm's length .... **Group C** (p. 22)

3. Inflorescence a well-developed panicle or a series of two to several unbranched or sparingly branched arms, each bearing a spike, raceme, or rame of spikelets; inflorescence branches easily seen at arm's length **4**

    4. Spikelets in repeating pairs, typically one sessile and the other pedicellate (sometimes both equally or unequally stalked); first glume firm to hard, clasping or enclosing the second glume; fertile lemma thin, membranous or translucent, its midnerve often extended into a prominent awn (Fig. 3D) ....
.... **Group D** (p. 34)

    4. Spikelets occurring singly at a node, infrequently in pairs or trios; if paired, the glumes and lemmas not as above **5**

5. Inflorescence a series of two or more unbranched or sparingly branched arms, each bearing a spike or raceme of spikelets
.... **Group E** (p. 37)

5. Inflorescence a well-developed panicle of few to many branches that are themselves branched and re-branched **6**

6. Spikelets with a single floret subtended by two glumes, one glume, or no glumes at all .... **Group F** (p. 43)

6. Spikelets with two or more florets (one or more sometimes reduced to sterile lemmas or awns) subtended by one or two glumes **7**

7. Spikelets with one or two glumes and two or more florets; if sterile lemmas present, these not noticeably different in texture from the fertile one(s) .... **Group G** (p. 49)

7. Spikelets with three membranous or papery outer bracts (a small first glume, which is sometimes missing; a larger second glume and a sterile lemma) and a single fertile floret, this typically hard and shiny (Fig. 31) .... **Group H** (p. 59)

KEY TO THE GRASSES OF GROUP A

1. Culms woody, the grasses bamboo-like; midculm region with axillary branches; inflorescence an axillary panicle or fascicle **2**
1. Culms tough and ± inflexible, but not woody; grasses not bamboo-like; midculm region without axillary branches; inflorescence terminal and plume-like **4**

   2. Leaf sheath apex with a series of bristles 2-10 mm long .... ***Arundinaria gigantea* (Walt.) Muhl.**[1] Cane or switch cane. Common native bamboo of the southeastern U.S. (27)[2]

   2. Leaf sheath without bristles **3**

3. Mature culms 1-2 cm in diameter; axillary branches solitary or rarely paired at a node .... ***Pseudosasa japonica* Makino.**[3] Arrow bamboo or metake. Escaped ornamental in Florida.
3. Mature culms 3 to several cm in diameter; axillary branches few to several at a node .... ***Bambusa vulgaris* Schrad. ex J. C. Wendl.**[3] Common bamboo. Escaped ornamental in Florida.

   4. Spikelets with a single well-developed floret **5**

   4. Spikelets with several well-developed florets **9**

5. Spikelets awnless **6**
5. Spikelets awned **8**

   6. Spikelets subtended by a conspicuous bristle .... ***Setaria magna* Griseb.** Giant bristlegrass. Marshes and wet areas of Atlantic and Gulf coasts. (724)

   6. Spikelets not subtended by a conspicuous bristle, but by long, silky hairs **7**

7. Leaf blades 4-6 cm wide; culms 2-3 cm in diameter, their lower portions prominently jointed .... ***Saccharum officinarum* L.** Sugar cane. Escaped crop plant in Southern states, especially Louisiana. (740)

7. Leaf blades about 1 cm wide; culms about 1 cm in diameter, their lower portions not prominently jointed .... ***Miscanthus*** Eulalia. Escaped ornamental in the eastern U.S. and Iowa. (739)

8. Spikelets paired, one sessile and the other stalked, the sessile spikelet falling with the pedicel and a section of rachis ... . **Erianthus** Plumegrass. Wet and marshy areas of the eastern and southern states. (743)

8. Spikelets paired, unequally stalked, and falling separately from the rachis .... **Miscanthus** Eulalia. Escaped ornamental in the eastern U.S. and Iowa. (739)

9. Lemmas glabrous .... **Phragmites australis (Cav.) Trin. ex Steud.**[4] Common reed. Widespread in wet areas. (190)

9. Lemmas hairy **10**

10. Glumes 3-nerved .... **Arundo donax L.** Giant reed. Used along waterways for erosion control and as an ornamental, mostly in the eastern and southern states. (184)

10. Glumes 1-nerved **11**

11. Lemma back glabrous, the margins ciliate .... **Neyraudia reynaudiana (Kunth) Keng.** Escaped ornamental in southern Florida. (190)

11. Lemma back clothed in long hairs .... **Cortaderia**[5] Pampasgrass. Ornamentals in the warmer parts of the country; one species a pernicious weed along the northern California coast. (189)

KEY TO THE GRASSES OF GROUP B

1. Some spikelets of the inflorescence modified into hard, bony or spiny structures **2**
1. Spikelets not modified into hard, bony or spiny structures .. **4**

    2. Spikelets bur-like, partially hidden by enveloping leaves ....
    .... **Buchloë dactyloides (Nutt.) Engelm.**
    Buffalo grass. Important range plant of the Great Plains, especially the short grass prairie. (545)
    2. Spikelets hard and shiny, but not bur-like **3**

3. Pistillate spikelet one per inflorescence branch, gray-white, very hard and shiny at maturity .... **Coix lacryma-jobi L.**
Job's tears. Escaped ornamental in Florida. The seed-like fruiting involucres are incorporated into jewelry. (790)
3. Pistillate spikelets two to several per branch, these golden-brown at maturity .... **Tripsacum**
Gamagrass. Maize relatives found in Arizona, Florida, and much of the eastern U.S. (790)

    4. Plants more than 1.5 m tall **5**
    4. Plants less than 1 m tall **7**

5. Plants terrestrial; staminate and pistillate spikelets in separate inflorescences on different parts of the plant, the staminate ones terminal and the pistillate ones axillary .... **Zea**[6]
Maize, corn, teosinte. Although maize does not persist outside of cultivation, teosinte has escaped and is established. (792 & 794)
5. Plants aquatic or semiaquatic; staminate and pistillate spikelets occurring in the same inflorescence **6**

    6. Staminate and pistillate spikelets intermixed on the same panicle branches ....
    .... **Zizaniopsis miliacea (Michx.) Doell & Aschers.**
    Southern wildrice. Wet places in the southeastern U.S. (563)
    6. Pistillate spikelets on ascending branches; staminate ones on spreading lower branches of the same inflorescence ......
    .... **Zizania**
    Wildrice. One species, commercial wildrice, is found in marshes in the eastern U.S.; a second is endemic in Texas. (561)

GROUP B

7. Inflorescence of some, if not all, completely sterile spikelets ...
.... **8**
7. Inflorescence of staminate and/or pistillate spikelets, no completely sterile spikelets present **10**

    8. Inflorescence of spikelets with several tiny bulblets, these bearing conspicuous purplish, awn-like tails .. ***Poa bulbosa* L.** Bulbous bluegrass. Fields and meadows of Atlantic, central, and western states. (122)

    8. Inflorescence a mixture of fertile and sterile spikelets ... **9**

    9. Fertile floret one, on a short stalk within the fertile spikelet ....
.... ***Lamarckia aurea* (L.) Moench.** Goldentop. Disturbed places, mostly in Texas, Arizona, and California. (184)

    9. Fertile florets two or three, these sessile within the fertile spikelet
.... ***Cynosurus*** Dogtail. Mediterranean introductions at several sites in the U.S. (183)

       10. Pistillate spikelet conspicuously awned ....
.... ***Scleropogon brevifolius* Phil.** Burro grass. Semiarid plains, Colorado to Texas, Nevada, and Arizona. (228)

       10. Pistillate spikelet awnless **11**

11. Aquatic or semiaquatic grasses of the Southeast ...... ***Luziola*** (565)
11. Plants of sand flats in Texas ....
.... ***Allolepis texana* (Vasey) Soders. & Decker.** Saltgrass. (177)

KEY TO THE GRASSES OF GROUP C

1. Mature inflorescence a head-like cluster or spike partially hidden by enveloping leaves; plants low, often less than 1 dm tall **2**
1. Mature inflorescence well-exserted from the leaf sheaths; plants typically taller than 1 dm **9**

    2. Glumes absent **3**
    2. One or both glumes present **4**

3. Lemmas fan-shaped; vernal pools and alkali soils of interior California .... *Neostapfia colusana* **(Davy) Davy.** Endemic to a few counties in California. (218)
3. Lemmas not fan-shaped; coastal flats of California and the Gulf states .... *Monanthochloë littoralis* **Engelm.** Coastal habitats of California, Texas, Louisiana, and Florida. (175)

    4. Spikelets with a single floret; lemmas awnless **5**
    4. Spikelets with a few to several florets; lemmas awned or awnless
    .... **6**

5. Spikelets in bur-like clusters of two to four ....
.... *Buchloë dactyloides* **(Nutt.) Engelm.** Buffalo grass. Important range grass of the Great Plains, especially the short grass prairie. (545)
5. Spikelets in a tight panicle, but not in bur-like clusters .... *Crypsis*[8] Adventive in several widely scattered sites throughout the U.S. (432 & 433)

    6. Lemmas awnless .... *Sclerochloa dura* **(L.) Beauv.** Adventive in several widely scattered sites throughout the U.S. (93)
    6. Lemmas with one or three awns **7**

7. Lemmas with three ciliate awns .... *Blepharidachne* Two species in the U.S., one endemic in Texas and the other in arid parts of California, Nevada, and Utah. (222)
7. Lemmas with a single awn **8**

8. Glumes longer than the lemmas; lemmas bifid (except in *Erioneuron pilosum*) .... ***Erioneuron***[9]
Fluffgrass, hairy tridens. Arid regions of the Southwest. (207)

8. Glumes shorter than the lemmas, lemmas narrowing to a point .... ***Monroa squarrosa* (Nutt.) Torr.**[10]
False buffalo grass. A grass of the western states. (544)

9. Inflorescence a mixture of sterile and fertile spikelets, these very different in appearance **10**

9. All spikelets similar and fertile **14**

10. Spikelets in groups of seven, one fertile surrounded by six sterile; glumes winged .... ***Phalaris paradoxa* L.**
Introduction in grain fields of California, Arizona, Louisiana, and Pennsylvania. (551)

10. Spikelets in pairs, trios, or fascicles; glumes not winged ...
.... **11**

11. Inflorescence dense, 1-sided, with drooping clusters of spikelets
.... ***Lamarckia aurea* (L.) Moench.**
Goldentop. Disturbed sites in Texas, Arizona, and California. (184)

11. Inflorescence erect and spike-like or a capitate, somewhat 1-sided panicle **12**

12. Perfect florets two or three per fertile spikelet; spikelets paired at a node .... ***Cynosurus***
Dogtail. Mediterranean introduction at several locations in the U.S. (183)

12. Perfect floret one per fertile spikelet; spikelets three per node
.... **13**

13. Stoloniferous or rhizomatous perennials; lemmas awnless ......
.... ***Hilaria***
Curly mesquite, galleta, or tobosa grass. Deserts and semiarid regions of the Southwest. (485)

13. Annuals or perennials, but stolons or rhizomes lacking; lemma with a conspicuous terminal awn .... ***Hordeum***
Barley. Crop plant and widely distributed weeds. (267)

14. Lemmas with five or more awns or awn-like lobes **15**

14. Lemmas with no more than three awns or awn-like lobes
.... **17**

15. Lemmas with five awns or lobes .... *Orcuttia*
Mostly endemic in vernal pools of the Central Valley in California.
(220)
15. Lemmas with 9-11 awns **16**

    16. Awns plumose .... *Enneapogon desvauxii* **Beauv.**
    Spike pappusgrass. Arid sites in the West and Southwest. (227)
    16. Awns glabrous to scabrous, but not plumose ....
    .... *Pappophorum.*
    Pappusgrass. Grasslands of the Southwest. (225)

17. Inflorescence a dense, 1-sided spike or a series of spreading to
appressed 1-sided spikes inserted along a central axis ... **18**
17. Inflorescence an erect, balanced spike, spike-like panicle, or spike-
like raceme **24**

    18. Culms bearing a series of lateral 1-sided spikes inserted along a
    central axis .... *Spartina*
    Cordgrass. Coastal saltmarshes and interior wet sites. (508)
    18. Culms bearing a single 1-sided spike **19**

19. Second glume with a rigid awn .... *Ctenium*
Toothache grass. Two species, one endemic in Florida and the other
more widespread in the Southeast. (514)
19. Second glume awnless (sometimes with a short point) **20**

    20. Spikelet with a single floret **21**
    20. Spikelet with two or more florets **23**

21. First glume missing; second glume reduced or missing ....
.... *Nardus stricta* **L.**
Sandy places, northeastern states and Oregon. (277)
21. Both glumes present and well-developed **22**

    22. Lemmas 5-nerved .... *Mibora minima* **(L.) Desv.**
    Known only from Plymouth, Massachusetts. (354)
    22. Lemmas 3-nerved, the lateral ones sometimes faint ....
    .... *Microchloa kunthii* **Desv.**
    Known only from southern Arizona. (501)

23. Spikelets with staminate florets only ....
.... *Buchloë dactyloides* (Nutt.) **Engelm.**
Buffalo grass. Important range plant of the Great Plains, especially
the short grass prairie. (545)

23. Spikelets with perfect florets .... *Bouteloua*[11]
Grama grass. Mostly in the drier parts of the West and Southwest. (532)

24. Spikelets subtended by a series of bristles or enclosed in a spiny
or bristly involucre **25**

24. Spikelets not subtended by a series of bristles or enclosed in a
spiny or bristly involucre **27**

25. Spikelets enclosed in an involucre bearing straight or curved spines
(infrequently softer bristles) .... *Cenchrus*
Sandbur. Widely scattered across the country in disturbed, often
sandy sites. (730)

25. Spikelets subtended by a series of separate bristles **26**

26. Spikelets disarticulating without the subtending bristles .....
.... *Setaria*[12]
Foxtail or bristlegrass. Widely occurring throughout the U.S.,
often in agricultural areas and disturbed sites. (718)

26. Spikelets disarticulating with the subtending bristles attached
.... *Pennisetum*
Fountain grass, feathertop, and pearl millet. Mostly in the
Southeast, but widely planted and escaping. (727)

27. Glumes bearing hooked barbs .... *Tragus*
Cocklebur grass. Mostly weedy at a few sites along the Atlantic
Coast states and in the Southwest. (482)

27. Glumes without hooked barbs **28**

28. Spikelets ± sunken in the cavities or pits of a thickened rachis
.... **29**

28. Spikelets clearly visible, not sunken in a thickened rachis
.... **39**

29. Spikelets awned **30**

29. Spikelets awnless **31**

30. Glumes awnless; floret one per spikelet . . . .
. . . . **Scribneria bolanderi (Thurb.) Hack.**
Sandy places, Washington to California. (279)

30. Glumes with 1-4 awns; florets two to five per spikelet . . . .
. . . . **Aegilops**[13]
Goatgrass. Widespread weeds. (245)

31. Rachis and pedicel hairy . . . . **Elionurus**[14]
Balsamscale. Mostly in the Southeast and Southwest. (781)

31. Rachis and pedicel, if the latter present, glabrous **32**

32. Inflorescence distinctly flattened **33**

32. Inflorescence round in cross-section **35**

33. Glumes soft and flexible . . . .
. . . . **Stenotaphrum secundatum (Walt.) Kuntze.**
St. Augustine grass. Important lawngrass in the Southeast. (585)

33. Glumes hard and relatively inflexible **34**

34. First glume with a membranous fringe at its notched apex
. . . . **Eremochloa ophiuroides (Munro) Hack.**
Centipede grass. Lawngrass of the Southeastern U.S. (787)

34. First glume without an apical fringe and notch . . . .
. . . . **Hemarthria altissima (Poir.) Stapf & Hubb.**[15]
Ponds and ditches of southern Texas. (785)

35. Grasses of coastal mud flats and salt marshes **36**

35. Grasses of open ground, pine woods, and waste places . . **37**

36. Both glumes present, appearing as a single split one; lemma
1-nerved . . . . **Parapholis incurva (L.) C.E. Hubb.**
Sickle grass. Coastal marshes of the Atlantic, Gulf, and Pacific
states. (279)

36. One glume present; lemma 3-nerved . . . .
. . . . **Monerma cylindrica (Willd.) Coss. & Dur.**
Thintail. Adventive in California salt marshes. (277)

37. Sheaths glabrous or with soft hairs . . . . **Coelorachis**[16]
Necklace grass. Mostly in pine woodlands of the Southeast. (785)

37. Sheaths with coarse hairs, these sometimes irritating when touched
. . . . **38**

38. Leaf blade with a prominent white midrib ....
.... ***Rottboellia exaltata* L. f.**
Introduced sparingly in Florida. (783)
38. Leaf blade without a prominent white midrib ....
.... ***Hackelochloa granularis* (L.) Kuntze.**
Weedy places in Arizona, New Mexico, and several states in the
Southeast. (788)

39. Spikelets in clusters of four, their glumes fused to form a pitcher-
shaped, false involucre ....
.... ***Anthephora hermaphrodita* (L.) Kuntze.**
Escape from experimental gardens in Florida. (484)
39. Spikelets 1-3 per node (rarely four or more); glumes not united to
form a false involucre **40**

   40. Spikelets two or more per node **41**
   40. Spikelets one per node **57**

41. Flowering culms with both terminal and axillary inflorescences
.... ***Schizachyrium***[17]
Bluestem grass. Grasslands throughout most of the U.S. (749)
41. Flowering culms with terminal inflorescences only **42**

   42. Glumes minute or missing .... ***Hystrix***
   Bottlebrush grass. Wooded sites in California and much of the
   eastern U.S. (264)
   42. One or both glumes well-developed **43**

43. Glumes awnless **44**
43. Glumes awned **50**

   44. Spikelets with two to several fertile florets .... ***Elymus***
   Wildrye. Widespread perennials in a variety of habitats. (247)
   44. Spikelets sterile or with only one fertile floret **45**

45. Spikelets three per node, the central one sessile and the lateral ones
stalked **46**
45. Spikelets two per node, one sessile and the other stalked ....
.... **47**

46. Lemmas 5-nerved (these often faint), terminating in a single awn
.... *Hordeum*
Barley. Crop plant and widely occurring weeds. (267)
46. Lemmas 3-nerved, terminating in three awns ....
.... *Cathestecum erectum* **Vasey & Hack.**
Arid hills of Texas and Arizona. (543)

47. Spikelets awnless **48**
47. Spikelets awned **49**

48. Spikelets 3-4 mm long, the hairs at the base twice or three times
as long .... *Imperata*
Satintail or cogon grass. Scattered sites in the Southeast,
Southwest, and Oregon. (737)
48. Spikelets 6-8 mm long, ciliate to woolly, but the hairs no longer
than the spikelet .... *Elionurus*[14]
Balsamscale. Mostly in the Southeast and Southwest. (781)

49. Racemes 4-7 cm long; sessile spikelet perfect ....
.... *Heteropogon*
Tanglehead. Dry hills, pine woods, and waste places of the South-
east and Southwest. (779)
49. Racemes 10 cm or more long; pedicellate spikelet perfect ....
.... *Trachypogon*
Crinkle-awn. Hills and canyons of Texas, Arizona, and New
Mexico. (781)

50. Glumes bearing a lateral awn from about the middle ......
.... *Hilaria*
Curly mesquite, tobosa, galleta. Desert areas of the Southwest.
(485)
50. Glumes bearing one or more terminal awns **51**

51. Palea with two awns .... *Aegopogon tenellus* **(DC.) Trin.**
Mountains of southern Arizona. (489)
51. Palea awnless **52**

52. Rachis remaining intact at maturity **53**
52. Rachis breaking apart at maturity **57**

53. Lemmas 3-nerved **54**
53. Lemmas 5-nerved **55**

54. First glume 2- or 3-awned; lemma awn 2-3 mm long .... **Lycurus phleoides HBK.** Wolftail. Plains and rocky hills of the Southwest; adventive in Maine. (365)

54. First glume 1-awned; lemma awn 5-10 mm long .... **Taeniatherum caput-medusae (L.) Nevski**[18] Medusa head. Weedy in Idaho and the Pacific states from Washington to northern California. (250)

55. Fertile florets two to several per spikelet; plants perennial .... **Elymus** Wildrye. Widely occurring throughout the U.S. (247)

55. Fertile floret one per spikelet; robust annual crop .... **Hordeum vulgare L.** Barley. Escape from grain fields. (274)

56. Spikelets three per node; the central one with a single fertile floret .... **Hordeum** Barley. Widely distributed weedy plants. (267)

56. Spikelets typically two per node; fertile florets two or more per spikelet .... **Sitanion** Squirreltail. Open, rocky places of western states. (262)

57. Spikelets with a single floret, no reduced florets or sterile lemmas present **58**

57. Spikelets with two or more florets, these sometimes very small and easily overlooked (do a very careful dissection!) **69**

58. Glumes plumose or with conspicuous hairs on the keels (except in *Alopecurus myosuroides*) **59**

58. Glumes glabrous to sparsely pubescent, but not plumose, nor with conspicuous hairs on the keels **61**

59. Inflorescence a compact, cylindrical spike-like panicle, the branches scarcely evident **60**

59. Inflorescence a dense woolly panicle, taller than broad, its branches more evident .... **Lagurus ovatus L.** Hare's tail. Escape from cultivation as an ornamental at scattered localities. (369)

60. Glumes awned .... *Phleum*
Timothy. Widely scattered throughout the U.S. (367)
60. Glumes awnless .... *Alopecurus*
Foxtail. Occurring throughout the U.S. (358)

61. First glume absent .... *Zoysia*
Zoysia or Japanese lawngrass. Escaped lawngrass, mostly in the
Southeast. (484)
61. Both glumes present **62**

62. Glumes awned **63**
62. Glumes awnless **65**

63. First glume 2- or 3-awned .... *Lycurus phleoides* **HBK.**
Wolftail. Plains and rocky hills of Utah, Colorado, Oklahoma, Texas,
Arizona, and New Mexico. (365)
63. First glume 1-awned **64**

64. Awn several times longer than the body of the lemma (except in
Polypogon elongata); disarticulation below the glumes .....
.... *Polypogon*
Rabbitfoot grass. One species native to Arizona and California,
the other species introduced or adventive throughout the
U.S. (362)
64. Awn no longer than the body of the lemma (except in *Muhlen-
bergia glomerata* and *M. racemosa*); disarticulation above the
glumes .... *Muhlenbergia*
Muhly. Mainly western grasses, but several in the East and
Midwest. (369)

65. Second glume 4-5 times longer than the lemma ....
.... *Gastridium ventricosum* **(Gouan) Schinz & Thell.**
Nitgrass. A common weed in Oregon and California; also in Texas
and Massachusetts. (368)
65. Second glume typically only slightly longer than (rarely twice as long
as) the lemma **66**

66. Lemma awned from the middle or below, the awn slender and
often geniculate .... *Calamagrostis*
Reedgrass. Many species of local distribution, while others are
widely occurring in wet habitats in the northern states. (313)
66. Lemmas awnless or if awned, from the apex **67**

67. Coarse grasses of coastal dunes; spikelets 1 cm or more long; lemmas 5- to 7-nerved .... ***Ammophila*** Beach grass. Atlantic states, Great Lakes, and introduced on sand dunes of the Pacific coast. (329)

67. Grasses of interior sites; spikelets less than 0.5 cm long; lemmas 1- or 3-nerved **68**

    68. Lemmas 1-nerved; throat of the leaf sheath often hairy ... . ***Sporobolus*** Dropseed. Sandy soils and alkali sites throughout the U.S. (413)

    68. Lemmas 3-nerved; throat of the leaf sheath not noticeably hairy .... ***Muhlenbergia*** Muhly. Mainly western grasses, but several in the East and Midwest. (369)

69. Fertile floret one, subtended by two (rarely one) greatly reduced sterile florets, these easily overlooked (do a careful dissection!) **70**

69. Florets two or more, more than one of which is often fertile; if reduced, sterile florets present, these above the fertile one(s) **71**

    70. Sterile florets reduced to small, awnless scale-like lemmas .... ***Phalaris*** Canary grass. Widely distributed, many of them weedy. (551)

    70. Sterile florets reduced to hairy lemmas with awns exceeding the fertile floret .... ***Anthoxanthum*** Vernal grass. Meadows, pastures, and waste places, mostly in the eastern U.S. and in the Pacific states. (549)

71. Lemmas 3-nerved **72**

71. Lemmas 5- to several-nerved **75**

    72. Spikelets unisexual, the species monoecious or dioecious **73**

    72. Spikelets perfect **74**

73. Spikelet 1 cm or less long ...... ***Eragrostis reptans* Michx.**[19] Creeping lovegrass. Wet and sandy places, S. Dakota to Texas, Louisiana; Florida. (148)

73. Spikelets 2-3 cm long .... ***Scleropogon brevifolius* Phil.** Burro grass. Semiarid places, mostly in the Southwest. (227)

74. Leaf blades flat; glumes ± equal in length; lemma base glabrous
.... *Tridens*[20]
Woodlands and dry slopes, mostly in the eastern and southern
states. (207)

74. Leaf blades needle-like; glumes unequal in length; lemma with a
tuft of hairs at the base ....
.... *Tripogon spicatus* **(Nees) Ekman.**
Rocky hillsides in Texas. (497)

75. Nerves of the lemma parallel, not converging at the lemma apex
.... *Lophochlaena*[21]
Semaphore grass. Wet places and grassy areas of Washington,
Oregon, and California. (94)

75. Nerves of the lemma converging toward the apex **76**

76. Spikelets (except for the terminal one) with the inner glume
missing .... *Lolium*
Ryegrass. Pasture grasses and weedy species throughout the
U.S. (274)

76. Spikelets with both glumes present **77**

77. Spikelets on short pedicels **78**

77. Spikelets sessile **83**

78. Stout, rhizomatous-stoloniferous perennials with woody bases
and distichous leaves ....
.... *Swallenia alexandrae* **(Swallen) Soders. & Decker.**[22]
Known only from sand dunes in Inyo Co., California. (995)

78. Annuals or perennials; leaves not distichous; plants widely distributed in a variety of habitats **79**

79. Palea colorless; glumes unlike in shape, the second wider than the
first (do a very careful dissection!) .... *Koeleria*
June grass. Prairies and open woodlands throughout the U.S. (281)

79. Palea green or light brown; glumes similar in shape, equal or unequal
in length **80**

80. Spikelets awnless .... *Poa*
Bluegrass. Common grasses throughout much of the country,
especially in the western states and the Rocky Mountains. (99)

80. Spikelets awned **81**

81. Both glumes shorter than the florets .... **Vulpia**[23]
Annual fescue. Widely distributed weedy grasses. (58)

81. One or both glumes as long as or longer than the florets .....
.... **82**

    82. First glume longer than the first floret; lemma awn flattened;
    florets three or more .... **Danthonia**
    Oatgrass or poverty oats. Open, rocky, and wooded areas
    across the country. (307)

    82. First glume shorter than the first floret; lemma awn round in
    cross-section; florets two (rarely three or four) ....
    .... **Trisetum**
    Meadows, woods, and waste places in various regions of the
    country. (287)

83. Lemma keel ciliate .... **Secale**
Rye. Escaped crop plants in agricultural areas. (246)

83. Lemma keel not ciliate **84**

    84. Crop plant; spikelets ± turgid, glumes hard ..... **Triticum**
    Wheat. Escaped crop in agricultural areas. (243)

    84. Native and weedy grasses; spikelets not turgid; glumes not
    noticeably hard **85**

85. Palea margins prominently toothed or ciliate ....
.... **Brachypodium**
False brome. Adventive at scattered sites in California, Oregon, and
New Jersey. (56)

85. Palea margins entire **86**

    86. Plants annual; spikes less than 2 cm long ....
    .... **Eremopyrum triticeum (Gaertn.) Nevski.**[24]
    Annual wheatgrass. Introduced in Washington, Montana,
    Wyoming, and Idaho. (232)

    86. Plants perennial; spikes two to several cm long **87**

87. Glumes narrowly lanceolate; rachilla twisted at base so that the lemmas are 90° out of their normal position, the florets thus not
appearing 2-ranked .... **Elymus**[25]
Wildrye. Widely distributed throughout the U.S. (247)

87. Glumes narrowly lanceolate to broader; rachilla not twisted, the
florets 2-ranked .... **Agropyron**
Wheatgrass. Widely distributed in the western and northern
states. (230)

KEY TO THE GRASSES OF GROUP D

1. Inflorescence a series of several short racemes, each with a whorl of four staminate or sterile spikelets and a subtending spathe at its base .... **Themeda quadrivalvis (L.) Kuntze.** Kangaroo grass. Adventive on bottom lands in Landry Parish, Louisiana. (789)
1. Inflorescence various, but not a series of short, spathulate racemes with whorls of staminate or sterile spikelets at their bases **2**

2. Spikelets in trios **3**
2. Spikelets in pairs, the stalked one sometimes suppressed **4**

3. Erect annual 60-120 cm tall; trios of one sessile and two stalked spikelets .... **Chrysopogon pauciflorus (Chapm.) Benth. ex Vasey.** Sandy woods and open places in Florida. (779)
3. Stoloniferous, mat-forming perennial about 30 cm tall; trios of two sessile and one stalked spikelet .... **Polytrias amaura (Buse ex Miquel) Kuntze.**[3] Adventive near Miami, Florida.

4. Stalked spikelet of the pair completely suppressed, with only the pedicel remaining **5**
4. Stalked spikelet present, either similar to the sessile one or reduced **7**

5. Low, creeping annual; leaf blade with a cordate-clasping base .... **Arthraxon hispidus (Thunb.) Makino.** Pastures, lawns, and open ground, mostly in the Southeast. (748)
5. Erect perennials; leaf blades not cordate-clasping **6**

6. Inflorescences terminal only; first glume hirsute .... **Sorghastrum** Indian grass. Prairies east of the Rocky Mountains and woods in the Southeast. (775)
6. Inflorescences both terminal and axillary; first glume glabrous .... **Andropogon**[26] Bluestem. Prairies and sandy sites, mostly in the Southeast. (749)

7. Sessile and stalked spikelets both perfect **8**
7. Sessile spikelet perfect, the stalked one staminate or sterile ...
.... **11**

   8. Spikelets surrounded by a conspicuous tuft of soft hairs; inflorescence branches numerous **9**
   8. Spikelets not surrounded by a tuft of hairs; inflorescence branches 2-6 ....
.... *Microstegium vimineum* **(Trin.) A. Camus.**
Adventive in Pennsylvania, Ohio, and several states in the Southeast. (746)

9. Rachis shattering at maturity, spikelets falling in pairs with segments of the rachis still attached .... *Erianthus*
Plumegrass. Wet and marshy areas of the eastern and southern states. (743)
9. Rachis remaining intact at maturity, spikelets falling without attached rachis segments **10**

   10. Panicle several times longer than broad, its branches appressed .... *Imperata*
Satintail or cogon grass. Scattered sites in the Southeast, Southwest, and Oregon. (737)
   10. Panicle about as broad as long, its branches spreading ...
.... *Miscanthus*
Eulalia. Escaped ornamental in the eastern U.S. and Iowa. (739)
11. Inflorescence branches two to a few (about six) per panicle ..
.... **12**
11. Inflorescence branches numerous in each panicle **13**

   12. Sessile spikelet of the basal pair of an inflorescence branch awned .... *Andropogon*[26]
Bluestem. Prairies and sandy sites, mostly in the Southeast. (749)
   12. Sessile spikelet of the basal pair of an inflorescence branch awnless .... *Hyparrhenia rufa* **(Nees) Stapf.**
Escaped from cultivation in Florida. (772)

13. Spikelets awnless **14**
13. Spikelets awned **15**

14. Plants rhizomatous .... **Sorghum halepense (L.) Pers.**
Johnson grass. Escaped crop plant and pernicious weed in the
warmer parts of the U.S. (773)

14. Plants densely tufted .... **Vetiveria zizanioides (L.) Nash.**
Vetiver. Escaped from cultivation in Louisiana. (772)

15. Inflorescence a well-developed, much-branched panicle; pedicels
glabrous .... **Sorghum**
Sorghum and Johnson grass. Escaped crop plant and aggressive
weed in the warmer agricultural areas of the country. (773)

15. Inflorescence a series of unbranched or sparingly banched racemes
forming a panicle; pedicels conspicuously bearded **16**

16. Upper pedicels and rachis internodes with a central groove or
membranous area .... **Bothriochloa**[27]
Bluestem. Grasslands and rocky places, mostly in the southern
half of the U.S. (749)

16. Upper pedicels and rachis internodes rounded to flattened, but
without a central groove or thinner membranous area .....
.... **17**

17. Pedicellate spikelet tapering to a pointed apex ....
.... **Andropogon**[26]
Bluestem. Prairies and sandy sites, mostly in the Southeast. (749)

17. Pedicellate spikelet with a rounded apex .... **Dichanthium**[3]
Bluestem. Escaped forage grasses in southern Texas.

KEY TO THE GRASSES OF GROUP E

1. Both glumes missing, except in terminal spikelets of a branch
.... **Reimarochloa oligostachya (Munro) Hitchc.**
Wet places in Florida. (596)
1. One or both glumes present on all spikelets **2**

    2. Spikelets with two staminate florets, no perfect florets or sterile
lemma present ... **Buchloë dactyloides (Nutt.) Engelm.**[28]
Buffalo grass. Important range grass of the Great Plains,
especially the short grass prairie. (545)
    2. One or more perfect florets present **3**

3. Spikelets with a single fertile floret, no reduced florets present
.... **4**
3. Spikelets with one to several, well-developed and usually fertile
florets, together with one or more reduced florets (these sometimes
represented by sterile lemmas only) **11**

    4. Rachilla extended as a bristle beyond the point of insertion of the
floret (make a very careful dissection; the rachilla extension is
not immediately evident!) .... **Cynodon**
Bermuda grass. Pasture and lawn grass, escaping from cultivation and becoming weedy in the warmer parts of the U.S. (503)
    4. Rachilla not extended as a bristle **5**

5. Fertile lemma thick and rigid **6**
5. Fertile lemma thin and flexible, membranous to papery **8**

    6. Fertile lemma awned or mucronate; spikelets with a cup-like or
disk-like ring at their base .... **Eriochloa**
Cupgrass. Wet places of the Southeast and Southwest, and
occurring widely on the Great Plains. (587)
    6. Fertile lemma awnless and without a mucro; cup-like or disk-like
ring absent **7**

7. Spikelets narrowly oblong; fertile lemma with its rounded back facing
away from the rachis .... **Axonopus**
Carpetgrass. Moist places, woods, sandy, and disturbed sites, mostly
in the Southeast. (595)
7. Spikelets broadly ovate to oblong; fertile lemma with its back placed
toward the rachis .... **Paspalum**
Paspalum, Dallis grass, knot grass, bahia grass. Common native and
introduced grasses, mostly in the Southeast. (599)

8. Glumes with several distinct nerves .... *Digitaria*[29] Crabgrass. Mostly weedy grasses of disturbed sites. (573)
8. Glumes nerveless, 1- or 3-nerved **9**

9. Palea densely pubescent .... *Willkommia texana* **Hitchc.** Clay soils of wet areas in Texas. (504)
9. Palea more or less glabrous **10**

10. Inflorescence at least ½ to ¼ as long as the culm; disarticulation above the glumes ....
.... *Schedonnardus paniculatus* **(Nutt.) Trel.** Tumblegrass. Prairies and plains of the central states. (505)
10. Inflorescence less than ¼ the length of the culm; disarticulation below the glumes .... *Spartina* Cordgrass. Coastal marshes and interior wet sites. (508)

11. Spikelets with a single fertile floret **12**
11. Spikelets with two or more fertile florets **31**

12. Inflorescence a racemose series of short, stubby, spikes of two to several spikelets, these falling as a unit from an unbranched central axis **13**
12. Inflorescence often digitate; if racemose, then the branches well-developed and not disarticulating along with the spikelets from the unbranched central axis **15**

13. Spikelets in clusters of three, the central one perfect and the lateral ones staminate or sterile **14**
13. Spiklets not in clusters of three, if appearing so, then all alike and fertile .... *Bouteloua*[30] Grama grass. Prairies and more arid places, mostly in the Southwest. (532)

14. Glumes equal, notched, and awned ....
.... *Aegopogon tenellus* **(DC.) Trin.** Mountains of southern Arizona. (489)
14. Glumes unequal, not notched, and not awned ....
.... *Cathestecum erectum* **Vasey & Hitchc.** Dry hills of Texas and Arizona. (543)

15. Spikelets in pairs, trios, or fascicles; equally or unequally stalked **16**
15. Spikelets inserted singly on the rachis **19**

16. Fertile floret leathery to hard **17**
16. Fertile floret membranous to very delicate **18**

17. Spikelets awned .... *Echinochloa*
Barynard grass, jungle rice. Widespread weeds of moist places over much of the country. (711)
17. Spikelets awnless .... *Paspalum*
Paspalum, Dallis grass, knotgrass, bahia grass. Common native and introduced grasses, mostly in the Southeast. (599)

18. Spikelets awnless .... *Digitaria*
Crabgrass. Mostly weedy grasses of disturbed sites. (573)
18. Spikelets awned ....
.... *Alloteropsis cimicina* **(L.) Stapf in Prain.**[3]
Introduced in Florida.

19. Fertile floret leathery to hard, obviously different in texture from the softer glumes **20**
19. Fertile floret membranous to papery, its texture similar to that of the glumes **25**

20. First glume present on all spikelets **21**
20. First glume missing on most, if not all, spikelets **23**

21. Spikelet inserted so that its first glume is on the inside, adjacent to the rachis .... *Brachiaria*
Weedy annuals of the southern states. (592)
21. Spikelet inserted so that its first glume is on the outside, away from the rachis **22**

22. Fertile lemma obtuse, abruptly mucronate or short-awned ..
.... *Urochloa panicoides Beauv.*[3]
Occasional lawn weed in Dana Co., New Mexico.
22. Fertile lemma acute, but not mucronate or awned ....
.... *Paspalidium*[31]
Moist and aquatic sites, Florida, Louisiana, Texas, and Oklahoma. (680)

23. Fertile lemma awned or mucronate; spikelets with a cup-like or disk-like ring at their base .... *Eriochloa*
Cupgrass. Wet places of the Southeast and Southwest, and occurring widely in the Great Plains. (587)
23. Fertile lemma awnless; cup-like or disk-like ring absent ... **24**

24. Spikelet narrowly oblong; fertile lemma with its rounded back facing away from the rachis .... ***Axonopus*** Carpetgrass. Moist places, woods, sandy, and disturbed sites, mostly in the Southeast. (595)

24. Spikelets broadly ovate to oblong; fertile lemma with its back placed toward the rachis .... ***Paspalum*** Paspalum, Dallis grass, knotgrass, bahia grass. Common native and introduced grasses, mostly in the Southeast. (599)

25. Fertile lemma with several nerves .... ***Digitaria*** Crabgrass. Mostly weedy grasses of disturbed sites. (573)

25. Fertile lemma 3-nerved **26**

26. Arms of the inflorescence arising singly or in whorls along a central axis, the arms not digitate or clustered at the apex of the axis **27**

26. Arms of the inflorescence digitate or clustered at the apex of the central axis **29**

27. Central axis and arms of the inflorescence spikelet-bearing ... . ***Gymnopogon*** Skeleton grass. Sandy, wooded areas of the eastern states, with two species endemic in Florida. (516)

27. Central axis not spikelet-bearing **28**

28. Side branches one per node .... ***Bouteloua*** Grama grass. Prairies and more arid places, mostly in the Southwest. (532)

28. Side branches whorled, two or more per node .... ***Chloris***[32] Windmill grass, finger grass, Rhodes grass. Widespread native and weedy plants of the warmer parts of the U.S. (519)

29. Leaf sheaths rounded; blades often stiffly distichous .... ***Gymnopogon*** Skeleton grass. Sandy, wooded areas of the eastern states, with two species endemic in Florida. (516)

29. Leaf sheaths flattened, blades lax **30**

30. Second glume short-awned from between two lobes; lemma of the perfect floret mucronate or short-awned; spikelet dark brown at maturity .... ***Eustachys***[33] Windmill grass, finger grass. Wet places, sandy fields, and woods of the southeastern states to Texas. (519)

30. Second glume pointed to mucronate; lemma of the perfect floret conspicuously awned; spikelets remaining straw-colored at maturity .... ***Chloris***[32] Windmill grass, finger grass, Rhodes grass. Widespread native and weedy grasses of the warmer parts of the U.S. (519)

31. Arms of the inflorescence arising singly at different nodes along a central axis, the arms not digitate or clustered at the apex of the axis **32**

31. Arms of the inflorescence digitate or clustered at the apex of the central axis **38**

32. Lemmas with long-ciliate margins .... ***Trichoneura elegans* Swallen.** Silveus grass. Endemic in sandy soils of southern Texas. (496)

32. Lemmas with glabrous to somewhat hairy margins, but not long-ciliate **33**

33. Lemmas 3-nerved, sometimes appearing 1-nerved **34**

33. Lemmas 5- to several-nerved **36**

34. Throat of leaf sheaths densely hairy .... ***Eragrostis sessilispica* Buckl.** Plains and prairies of Kansas, Oklahoma, Texas, and New Mexico. (144)

34. Throat of leaf sheaths glabrous to slightly hairy **35**

35. Spikelets 4-12 mm long, with 5-12 florets; lemmas ± rounded .... ***Diplachne***[34] Sprangletop. Rocky hills, sandy or wet areas, mostly in the southern half of the country. (491)

35. Spikelets 1-4 mm long, with 2-5 (-7) florets; lemmas strongly keeled, appearing 3-angled .... ***Leptochloa***[35] Sprangletop. Rocky hills, sandy or wet sites, mostly in the southern half of the country. (491)

36. Second glume 7-nerved ... ***Sclerochloa dura* (L.) Beauv.**
Sandy or gravelly soils, mostly in scattered locations in the West. (93)

36. Second glume 3-nerved **37**

37. Lemmas mucronate or with a well-developed awn ... ***Vulpia***[36]
Annual fescue. Widely distributed weedy annuals. (57)

37. Lemmas without an awn or mucro ....
.... ***Catapodium rigidum* (L.) C.E. Hubb.**[37]
Waste places and fields at widely scattered locations. (76)

38. Glumes and lemmas awnless .... ***Eleusine***
Goosegrass and African millet. Common weed over much of the U.S. and sparingly escaped crop plant. (499)

38. Glumes and/or lemmas 1- or 3-awned **39**

39. Rachis of inflorescence branch extended as a point beyond the last spikelet .... ***Dactyloctenium aegyptium* (L.) Beauv.**
Crowfoot grass. Occasional weed through the southern half of the country. (501)

39. Rachis not extended as a point beyond the last spikelet ......
.... ***Chloris***
Windmill grass, finger grass, Rhodes grass. Widespread native and weedy plants of the warmer parts of the U.S. (519)

KEY TO THE GRASSES OF GROUP F

1. Spikelets unisexual; plants aquatic or semiaquatic **2**
1. Spikelets with a single perfect floret; plants of terrestrial habitats (sometimes marshy, moist, or wet sites) **4**

   2. Small aquatic plant with floating culms and leaves .... ***Hydrochloa caroliniensis* Beauv.** Ponds and streams, North Carolina to Florida. (566)
   2. Robust perennials with erect culms **3**

3. Staminate spikelets on spreading lower branches; pistillate spikelets on erect upper branches .... ***Zizania*** Wildrice. Marshy places of the eastern U.S., one species endemic in Texas. (561)
3. Staminate and pistillate spikelets intermixed on the same branches .... ***Zizaniopsis miliacea* (Michx.) Doell & Aschers.** Marshy places, Southeast to Texas and Oklahoma. (563)

   4. Glumes rudimentary or absent **5**
   4. Glumes present and well-developed **9**

5. Lemma with an awn 1-2 cm long .... ***Brachyelytrum erectum* (Schreb.) Beauv.** Moist or rocky woods of the eastern U.S. (433)
5. Lemma awnless or if awned, the awn not more than 0.5 cm long **6**

   6. Tufted perennial of alpine peaks .... ***Phippsia algida* (Phipps) R. Br.** Summits of alpine peaks in Colorado are the only known locations in the U.S. (354)
   6. Annuals or perennials of wet areas, mud flats, and mesic woodlands at low altitudes **7**

7. Annual grasses less than 5 cm tall; spikelets less than 2 mm long; known only from mud flats .... ***Coleanthus subtilis* (Tratt.) Siedel.** Mud flats of the Columbia River in Washington and Oregon. (354)
7. Plants typically 0.5 m or more tall; spikelets 4-10 mm long; crop plants or perennial natives of wet areas and mesic woodlands **8**

8. Spikelets 7-10 mm long; crop plant ..... ***Oryza sativa* L.** Rice. Adventive near the coast, Virginia to Florida and Texas; Central Valley of California. (556)
8. Spikelets less than 6 mm long; native grasses .... ***Leersia*** Catchfly grass, rice cutgrass, or whitegrass. Mostly in wet places of the eastern U.S. (558)

9. Spikelets ± circular; the firm, equal, prominently keeled glumes with transverse wrinkles ... ***Beckmannia syzigachne* (Steud.) Fern.** Sloughgrass. Marshes and ditches, mostly in the Northwest and North Central states. (508)
9. Spikelets not circular; the glumes, if keeled, not with transverse wrinkles **10**

10. Spikelets awnless or nearly so **11**
10. Spikelets distinctly awned **22**

11. Lemma with a prominent tuft of hair at the base **12**
11. Lemma without a prominent tuft of hair at the base **15**

12. Coastal plants with dense panicles; spikelets mostly 10-15 mm long .... ***Ammophila*** Beachgrass. Atlantic states, Great Lakes, and introduced on sand dunes of the Pacific coast. (329)
12. Plants not restricted to coastal dunes; spikelets 3-8 mm long **13**

13. Lemma 3-nerved .... ***Muhlenbergia*** Muhly. Mainly western grasses, but several in the East and Midwest. (369)
13. Lemma 1-nerved or with five to several indistinct nerves .. **14**

14. Plants rhizomatous; glume 1-nerved; caryopsis spindle-shaped .... ***Calamovilfa*** Sand reedgrass. Marshy places in the East, sandy habitats in the North Central to Southwest. (329)
14. Plants not rhizomatous; glume 3- to 5-nerved; caryopsis spherical .... ***Oryzopsis*** Widely distributed in dry, open rocky sites and wooded areas. (437)

15. Both glumes as long as, or longer than, the lemma **16**
15. At least the first glume shorter than the lemma **19**

16. Glumes 5- to 7-nerved, the internerve region and margins with appressed, silky hairs .... ***Digitaria***[38] Fall witchgrass. Sandy hills and fields of the eastern, southeastern, and southwestern U.S. (585)

16. Glumes 1- or 3-nerved, appressed and silky hairs absent **17**

17. Fertile floret hard and shiny, dorsally compressed .... ***Milium effusum*** **L.** Damp or rocky woods of the northeastern states. (434)

17. Fertile floret soft and flexible, terete or laterally compressed **18**

18. Lemma 3-nerved; palea and lemma ± equal in length .... ***Muhlenbergia*** Muhly. Mainly western grasses, but several in the East and Midwest. (369)

18. Lemma 5-nerved, rarely 3-nerved; palea reduced or absent .... ***Agrostis*** Bentgrass, redtop, or thingrass. Widely distributed native and introduced grasses over most′ of the country. (334)

19. Lemma 5-nerved; stamens six .... ***Oryza sativa*** **L.** Rice. Adventive near the coast, Virginia to Florida and Texas; Central Valley of California. (556)

19. Lemma 1- or 3-nerved; stamens two or three **20**

20. Lemma 1-nerved .... ***Sporobolus*** Dropseed. Widely occurring grasses in a variety of habitats. (413)

20. Lemma 3-nerved **21**

21. Nerves of lemma densely hairy .... ***Blepharoneuron tricholepis*** **(Torr.) Nash.** Hairy dropseed. Mid to higher elevation conifer forests of Colorado and Utah to Texas and Arizona. (432)

21. Nerves of lemma glabrous to scabrous .... ***Muhlenbergia*** Muhly. Mainly western grasses, but several in the East and Midwest. (369)

22. Lemma awn 3-parted, the lateral branches sometimes much shorter than the central one (rarely obsolete) .... **Aristida** Three-awn, spider grass, beggartick grass, or arrowfeather. Sandy places in the East and Southeast; semiarid sites of the Southwest. (460)

22. Lemma awn not divided into three parts, rarely completely awnless **23**

23. Glumes awned **24**

23. Glumes awnless **27**

24. Glumes covered with long, silky hairs, rose when young and fading with age ....
.... **Rhynchelytrum repens (Willd.) C.E. Hubb.**[39] Natal or ruby grass. Sandy prairies, fields, and disturbed places in Florida, Texas, Arizona, and Calfornia. (716)

24. Glumes scabrous to glabrous, but not covered with long, silky hairs **25**

25. Glume awn several times longer than the body of the glume (except in *Polypogon elongatus*) .... **Polypogon** Rabbitfoot grass. One species native to California and Arizona, the other species introduced or adventive throughout the U.S. (362)

25. Glume awn shorter than the body of the glume (except in *Muhlenbergia glomerata* and *M. racemosa*) **26**

26. Palea less than 2/3 the length of the lemma, often obsolete.
.... **Agrostis** Bentgrass, redtop, and thin grass. Widely distributed native and introduced grasses over much of the U.S. (334)

26. Palea well-developed, typically as long as the lemma .....
.... **Muhlenbergia** Muhly. Mainly western grasses, but several in the East and Midwest. (369)

27. Escaped crop plant; stamens six .... **Oryza sativa L.** Rice. Adventive near the coast, Virginia to Florida and Texas; Central Valley of California. (556)

27. Native and introduced grasses; stamens two or three **28**

28. Lemma indurate, typically permanently enclosing the palea and caryopsis **29**

28. Lemma thin and flexible, not permanently enclosing the palea and caryopsis **32**

29. Lemma narrow; awn stout and persistent .... ***Stipa*** Needlegrass. Common plants in prairies and woodlands, mostly in the West. (445)

29. Lemma broad; awn slender and typically falling off after flowering **30**

30. Awn terminal or very nearly so; lemma not swollen on one side near the top .... ***Oryzopsis*** Ricegrass. Widely distributed in dry, open rocky sites and wooded areas. (437)

30. Awn not terminal, but inserted to one side; lemma swollen on one side near the top **31**

31. Palea without nerves or keel .... ***Nassella chilensis*** **(Trin. & Rupr.) E. Desv.**[3] Reported from ballast in Portland, Oregon. (443)

31. Palea prominently 2-keeled .... ***Piptochaetium fimbriatum*** **(HBK.) Hitchc.** Pinyon ricegrass. Open, rocky woods of Colorado, Arizona, New Mexico, and Texas. (443)

32. Lemma awned from or near its apex **33**

32. Lemma awned from the back or near the base **36**

33. Awn several times longer than the body of the lemma **34**

33. Awn no longer than the body of the lemma **35**

34. Lemma 2-toothed at the apex .... ***Limnodea arkansana*** **(Nutt.) L.H. Dewey.** Prairies and river banks, Coastal Plain, Florida to Texas; Arkansas and Oklahoma. (335)

34. Lemma apex pointed, not 2-toothed .... ***Apera*** Introduced at scattered locations across the U.S. (332)

35. Floret stipitate; rachilla extending beyond the palea as a minute bristle .... *Cinna* Woodreed. Moist woods over much of the U.S. (355)

35. Floret sessile; rachilla not forming a minute bristle above the palea .... *Muhlenbergia* Muhly. Mainly western grasses, but several in the East and the Midwest. (369)

36. Floret with a tuft of hair at the base; palea well-developed .... *Calamagrostis* Reedgrass. Many species of local distribution, while others are widely occurring in wet habitats in the northern states. (313)

36. Floret without a tuft of hair at the base; palea typically reduced or absent .... *Agrostis* Bentgrass, redtop, or thingrass. Widely distributed native and introduced grasses over much of the U.S. (334)

KEY TO THE GRASSES OF GROUP G

1. Spikelets two to several per node **2**
1. Spikelets one per node **3**

   2. Spikelets 3-5 per node, sessile; glumes ± equal in length
   .... ***Elymus***[40]
   Wildrye. Widespread perennials in a variety of habitats. (247)
   2. Spikelets two per node, stalked; first glume minute, the second
   well-developed .... ***Digitaria***[41]
   Sourgrass or cottontop. Dry and open areas in the Southeast
   and Southwest. (570)

3. Inflorescence a mixture of sterile and fertile spikelets, these quite
different in general structure **4**
3. Inflorescence of similar spikelets **5**

   4. Fertile spikelets with one perfect floret, this on a short stalk
   within the spikelet .... ***Lamarckia aurea* (L.) Moench.**
   Goldentop. Disturbed places; mostly in Texas, Arizona, and
   California. (184)
   4. Fertile spikelets with two or three perfect florets, these sessile
   within the spikelet .... ***Cynosurus***
   Dogtail. Mediterranean introduction at several sites across the
   U.S. (183)

5. Spikelets unisexual or sterile, no perfect floret(s) present ... **6**
5. Spikelets with one or more perfect florets **9**

   6. Florets modified into purple-based bulblets with long, awn-like
   tails .... ***Poa bulbosa* L.**[42]
   Bulbous bluegrass. Fields and meadows of the Atlantic, Central,
   and Western states. (122)
   6. Florets either staminate or pistillate **7**

7. Lemmas with a cottony or cobweb-like tuft of hairs at their bases
.... ***Poa***
Bluegrass. A large and diabolical group of native and introduced
grasses, widely occurring in the U.S. (99)
7. Lemmas without a cottony or cobweb-like tuft of hairs at their bases
.... **8**

8. Plants densely tufted; lemmas scabrous; grasses of dry, mountainous slopes ....
.... *Leucopoa kingii* **(S. Wats.) W.A. Weber.**[43]
Dry mountains and hills of Nebraska; Montana to Colorado; west to Oregon and Washington. (99)

8. Plants with horizontal, creeping rhizomes; lemmas glabrous; grasses of alkaline or saline sites ....
.... *Distichlis spicata* **(L.) Greene.**[44]
Saltgrass. Atlantic, Pacific, and Gulf coasts; interior alkaline and saline flats. (175)

9. Fertile floret one, accompanied by one or more staminate or sterile ones **10**

9. Fertile florets two or more **17**

10. Sterile florets inserted above AND below the fertile one ...
.... *Blepharidachne*
Dry places in California, Nevada, Utah, and Texas. (222)

10. Sterile florets inserted above OR below the fertile one ....
.... **11**

11. Sterile or staminate florets above the fertile one; the upper floret with a hooked or bent awn .... *Holcus*
Velvet grass. Open ground, meadows, and moist places; mostly in the East and Pacific states. (305)

11. Sterile floret(s) below the fertile one, these sometimes very small and easily overlooked (DO A VERY CAREFUL DISSECTION AT THIS POINT!) **12**

12. Fertile floret awned **13**

12. Fertile floret awnless **14**

13. Fertile floret subtended by one awned, staminate floret ....
.... *Arrhenatherum elatius* **(L.) Presl.**
Tall oatgrass. Escaped pasture grass on sandy soils in widely scattered locations. (303)

13. Fertile floret subtended by two awnless, staminate florets ......
.... *Ventenata dubia* **(Leers) Coss. & Durieu.**
Adventive in Idaho and Washington.

14. Lower florets reduced to sterile lemmas not exceeding half the length of the fertile floret .... ***Phalaris*** Canary grass. Widely distributed, many of them weedy. (551)

14. Lower staminate or sterile florets as long as or slightly longer than the fertile one **15**

15. Glumes unequal, the second noticeably longer than the first .. .. ***Anthoxanthum*** Vernal grass or sweet vernal grass. Meadows, pastures, and moist places, mostly in the eastern U.S. and in the Pacific states. (549)

15. Glumes ± equal **16**

   16. Glumes three-nerved .... ***Hierochloë*** Sweetgrass or holy grass. Meadows and forests of the northern, southwestern, and Pacific states. (547)

   16. Glumes 5- to several-nerved (look carefully) .... ***Ehrharta*** Escaped from cultivation at a few sites in California. (549)

17. Lemmas with five or more awns or awn-like lobes **18**

17. Lemmas awnless, one-awned, or three-awned **21**

   18. Lemmas with five awn-like lobes .... ***Orcuttia*** Endemic in vernal pools and wet depressions of the Central Valley of California. (220)

   18. Lemmas with nine or more awns or awn-like lobes ... **19**

19. Lemmas with nine plumose awns .... ***Enneapogon desvauxii*** **Beauv.** Spike pappusgrass. Arid sites in the West and Southwest. (227)

19. Lemmas with 11 or more glabrous to scabrous awns **20**

   20. Lemma apex a mixture of awns and awn-like teeth; glumes 5- to many-nerved .... ***Cottea pappophoroides*** **Kunth.** Plains and dry hills of Texas, New Mexico, and Arizona. (223)

   20. Lemma awns not intermixed with awn-like teeth; glumes one-nerved .... ***Pappophorum*** Pappusgrass. Grasslands of the Southwest. (225)

21. Lemmas three-awned **22**

21. Lemmas one-awned or awnless **23**

22. Lemmas glabrous; awns at least 3 cm long .... *Scleropogon brevifolius* **Phil.** Burro grass. Semiarid plains; Colorado to Texas, Nevada, and Arizona. (227)

22. Lemmas ciliate; awns less than 1 cm long .... *Blepharidachne* Dry places in California, Nevada, Utah, and Texas. (222)

23. Lemmas three-nerved, these usually prominent **24**

23. Lemmas 5- to many-nerved, these sometimes so faint that the lemmas may appear nerveless **32**

24. Nerves of the lemma hairy, at least on the lower part (excluding the callus) **25**

24. Nerves of the lemma glabrous, although the callus may be hairy **27**

25. Palea densely hairy on the upper half .... *Triplasis* Purple sandgrass. Dry, sandy sites of the Coastal Plain from N. Carolina to Florida and Mississippi; eastern U.S. (217)

25. Palea not densely hairy on the upper half **26**

26. Leaf blades with white margins; stigmas white .... *Erioneuron*[6] Fluffgrass or hairy tridens. Arid regions of the Southwest. (207)

26. Leaf blades not white-margined; stigmas purple .... *Tridens*[45] Purpletop or tridens. Wooded areas and dry slopes, mostly in the East and Southwest. (207)

27. Callus densely hairy ..... *Redfieldia flexuosa* **(Thurb.) Vasey.** Blowout grass. Sand hills, N. Dakota to Oklahoma and west to Utah and Arizona. (173)

27. Callus glabrous **28**

28. Second glume 3- to 5-nerved; caryopsis large, swollen, and beaked .... *Diarrhena americana* **Beauv.** Wooded areas, mostly in the eastern and central states. (171)

28. Second glume nerveless or one-nerved; caryopsis not especially large, nor turgid and beaked **29**

29. Spikelets ± terete; palea as long as or longer than the lemma
.... *Molinia caerulea* (L.) Moench.
Introduced in meadows and fields, Maine to Pennsylvania. (171)
29. Spikelets laterally compressed; palea shorter than the lemma ..
.... **30**

   30. Spikelets two-flowered; lemma with a squared apex ....
   .... *Catabrosa aquatica* (L.) Beauv.
   Brookgrass. Wet places, mostly in the western states. (169)
   30. Spikelets 3- to several-flowered; lemma apex pointed .....
   .... **31**

31. Panicle branches stout, widely and stiffly divergent; glumes signifi-
cantly firmer than the lemmas ....
.... *Cutandia memphitica* (Spreng.) **Richter.**
Introduced in the San Bernardino Mtns. of southern California.
(171)
31. Panicle branches slender to capillary, not widely and stiffly divergent;
glumes and lemmas of similar texture .... *Eragrostis*
Lovegrass. Widely occurring grasses, many of them weedy annuals.
(140)

   32. Some, if not all, of the lemmas awned **33**
   32. Lemmas awnless **50**

33. Lemmas 1.5 cm or more long **34**
33. Lemmas less than 1.2 cm long **35**

   34. Glumes longer than the lemmas; awn, if present, inserted on the
   back of the lemmas .... *Avena*
   Oats. Escaped crop plant and widely occurring weeds. (299)
   34. Glumes shorter than the lemmas; awn terminal ....
   .... *Bromus*[46]
   Brome grass. Native perennials and weedy annuals throughout
   the U.S. (52)

35. Lemmas awned from the base to a point 2/3 up the back ...
.... **36**
35. Lemmas awned from the apex, near the apex, or from between the
teeth of a bifid tip **40**

36. Spikelets with three to several florets; spikelets 1-1.5 cm long
.... *Helictotrichon*
Spike oat or alpine oat. Native and introduced species in scattered localities. (302)

36. Spikelets with two florets; spikelets mostly less than 1 cm long
.... **37**

37. Awn with an expanded, club-like apex; jointed and hairy at the middle
.... *Corynephorus canescens* **(L.) Beauv.**
Waste places in a few localities in the Northeast. (299)

37. Awn not expanded; not jointed and hairy at the middle ... **38**

38. Rachilla prolonged beyond the point of insertion of the upper floret **39**

38. Rachilla not prolonged .... *Aira*
Hairgrass. Weedy in the East, Southeast, and Pacific states. (297)

39. Awn inserted near the base of the lemma; lemma apex irregularly toothed .... *Deschampsia*[47]
Hairgrass. Mostly perennials of meadows in the western, north central, and eastern states. (292)

39. Awn inserted at the midpoint of the lemma; lemma apex tapering to a point .... *Vahlodea atropurpurea* **(Wahl.) Fr.**[48]
Mountain hairgrass. Woods and wet meadows; Pacific states, Idaho, Montana to Colorado, Maine, and New Hampshire. (294)

40. First glume longer than the lowest floret **41**

40. First glume no longer than the lowest floret **42**

41. Rachilla distinctly hairy .... *Trisetum*
Meadows, woods, and waste places in various regions of the country. (287)

41. Rachilla ± glabrous .... *Danthonia*
Oatgrass or poverty oats. Open, rocky, and wooded areas across the country. (307)

42. Glumes dissimilar in shape, the second wider than the first (spread them flat to make this comparison); first glume one-nerved, the second 3- to 5-nerved **43**

42. Glumes similar in shape, their nerve number the same ...
.... **44**

43. Second glume broadest above the middle ..... **Sphenopholis**
Wedgegrass or wedgescale. Woods, fields, and prairies over much of
the U.S. (283)

43. Second glume broadest below the middle .... **Koeleria**
June grass. Prairies and open woods throughout the country. (281)

44. Callus with long hairs ....
.... **Schizachne purpurascens (Torr.) Swallen.**
False melic. Rocky woods, mostly in the northern parts of the
country. (204)

44. Callus glabrous to scabrous **45**

45. Glumes papery; lemmas strongly nerved with a non-green, mem-
branous margin; underground bulbs often present ..... **Melica**
Onion grass or melic. Grasslands and mountain slopes, mostly of the
West. (190)

45. Glumes not papery; lemmas not strongly nerved; lemma margins not
thin and membranous; bulbs absent **46**

46. Lemma apex bifid; spikelets typically well over 1 cm long
.... **Bromus**
Brome grass. Native perennials and weedy annuals throughout
the U.S. (31)

46. Lemma apex entire; spikelets typically less than 1 cm long
.... **47**

47. Second glume as long or longer than the lowermost floret ....
.... **Trisetum**
Meadows, woods, and waste places in various regions of the
country. (287)

47. Second glume shorter than the lowermost floret **48**

48. Spikelets in dense, one-sided clumps at the ends of stiff panicle
branches; sheaths closed .... **Dactylis glomerata L.**
Orchard grass. Pasture grass and weedy over much of the U.S.
(182)

48. Spikelets not clustered at the tips of stiff panicle branches;
sheaths open **49**

49. Plants annual; stamens one per floret .... **Vulpia**[36]
Annual fescue. Widely distributed weedy annuals. (57)

49. Plants perennial; stamens three per floret .... **Festuca**[49]
Fescue. Widespread perennials. (57)

50. Glumes and lemmas inflated and papery, inserted at right angles to the rachilla .... *Briza* Quaking grass. Introduced at various locations across the country. (138)
50. Glumes and lemmas not inflated or papery, and not inserted at right angles to the rachilla **51**

51. Lowermost florets sterile **52**
51. Lowermost florets fertile **53**

   52. Spikelets light brown; plants of coastal dunes .... *Uniola paniculata* **L.**[50] Sea oats. Sand dunes; Virginia to Florida and Texas. (178)
   52. Spikelets green; plants of interior woodlands .... *Chasmanthium*[51] Native perennials of wooded areas, mostly in the Southeast. (178)

53. First glume distinctly longer than the lowermost lemma **54**
53. First glume no longer than the lowermost lemma **55**

   54. Lemmas 2-3 mm long .... *Schismus* Adventive annuals in Texas, New Mexico, Arizona, and California. (280)
   54. Lemmas 6 mm or more long .... *Sieglingia decumbens* **(L.) Bernh.** Introduced in Washington and California. (305)

55. Nerves of the lemma ± equally spaced and parallel, not converging toward the tip; nerves often prominent **56**
55. Nerves not ± equally spaced and parallel, but converging with one another at the tip of the lemma **57**

   56. Plants of saline areas; second glume three-nerved; lemmas five-nerved; sheaths open .... *Puccinellia*[52] Alkali grass. Wet sites, especially alkaline ones, in the cooler parts of the U.S. (77)
   56. Plants of wooded and freshwater sites; second glume one-nerved; lemmas 7- to 9-nerved; sheaths closed .... *Glyceria*[53] Mannagrass. Marshes and moist woodlands throughout the country. (81)

57. Glumes dissimilar in shape, the second wider than the first (spread them flat to make this comparison) **58**

57. Glumes similar in shape **59**

   58. Second glume broadest above the middle ....
   .... ***Sphenopholis***
   Wedgegrass or wedgescale. Woods, fields, and prairies over much of the U.S. (283)

   58. Second glume broadest below the middle .... ***Koeleria***
   June grass. Prairies and open woods throughout the U.S. (381)

59. Callus and/or lemma base bearded or clothed in a web of fine, cottony hairs **60**

59. Callus and/or lemma base not bearded or clothed in cottony hairs **61**

   60. First glume three-nerved, the second five-nerved; lemma apex irregularly cleft or torn ....
   .... ***Scolochloa festucacea* (Willd.) Link.**
   Wet places; Minnesota and Iowa, N. Dakota to Nebraska and Oregon. (93)

   60. First glume one-nerved, the second three-nerved; lemma apex acute or obtuse .... ***Poa***
   Bluegrass. A large and challenging group of native and introduced grasses occurring throughout the country. (99)

61. Lemmas five-nerved (sometimes appearing three-nerved because of the faintness of two intermediate nerves) **62**

61. Lemmas with seven or more nerves **64**

   62. Rachilla thickened and remaining attached to the florets at disarticulation; lemmas nearly terete ....
   .... ***Catapodium rigidum* (L.) C.E. Hubb. ex Dony.**[54]
   Adventive in Massachusetts, Florida to Mississippi, Texas, S. Dakota, and the Pacific states. (76)

   62. Rachilla not especially thickened and not remaining attached to the disarticulating florets; lemmas definitely flattened .. **63**

63. Leaf blades with folded tips, resembling the bow of a boat ...
   .... ***Poa***
   Bluegrass. A large and taxonomically frustrating group of native and introduced grasses found throughout the U.S. (99)

63. Leaf blades with flat, tapered tips .... ***Festuca***
   Fescue grass. Widespread perennials in a variety of habitats. (57)

64. Glumes papery; lemmas strongly nerved with a thin, non-green, membranous margin; underground bulbs often present .... *Melica*
Onion grass or melic. Grasslands and mountain slopes, mostly in the West. (190)

64. Glumes not papery; lemmas not strongly nerved; lemma margins not thin and membranous; bulbs absent **65**

65. Lemmas with a bifid apex; sheaths closed; spikelets typically well over 1.5 cm long .... *Bromus*
Brome grass. Native perennials and weedy annuals throughout the U.S. (31)

65. Lemmas tapering to a point; sheaths open; spikelets typically less than 1 cm long (except in *Vaseyochloa*) **66**

66. Palea margins winged ....
.... *Vaseyochloa multinervosa* **(Vasey) Hitchc.**
Restricted to sandy places in southern Texas. (207)

66. Palea margins not winged .... *Festuca*[49]
Fescue grass. Native and introduced perennials in a variety of habitats. (57)

KEY TO THE GRASSES OF GROUP H

1. Spikelets subtended by a single bristle or a series of bristles, or enclosed in a spiny or bristly involucre **2**
1. Spikelets not associated with bristles or enclosed in an involucre **6**

    2. Spikelets at the ends of branches subtended by a single bristle **3**
    2. Most, if not all, spikelets subtended by a series of bristles or spines, or enclosed in an involucre **4**

3. Spikelets awnless .... **Setaria**[55]
Foxtail or bristlegrass. Sandy places in Texas and Florida. (626)
3. Spikelets awned or awn-tipped .... **Echinochloa**
Barnyard grass and jungle rice. Widespread weeds of moist places over much of the U.S. (711)

    4. Spikelets enclosed in a spiny or bristly involucre, the spines typically substantial enough to be injurious .... **Cenchrus**[56]
    Sandbur. Widely scattered across the country in disturbed, often sandy sites. (730)
    4. Spikelets subtended by a series of ± separate bristles, these not modified into spines **5**

5. Subtending bristles remaining attached to the disarticulated spikelets .... **Pennisetum**
Fountain grass, elephant grass, kikuyu grass, pearl millet. Escaped ornamentals, lawn grasses, and forage plants in the warmer parts of the U.S. (727)
5. Subtending bristles not disarticulating with the spikelets, but remaining on the plant .... **Setaria**
Foxtail or bristlegrass. Widely occurring, often in agricultural and disturbed sites. (718)

    6. First glume awned or awnless; second glume awned (look very carefully!) **7**
    6. Both glumes awnless **9**

7. Both glumes well-developed; spikelets glabrous to scabrous ...
.... **8**

7. First glume minute; second glume and sterile lemma silky-hairy, rose
when young, fading with age ....
.... ***Rhynchelytrum repens* (Willd.) Hubb.**
Natal grass or ruby grass. Sandy prairies, fields, and disturbed places
in Florida, Texas, Arizona, and California. (716)

   8. First glume with an awn to three times the length of the body of the
   glume; glumes subequal in length .... ***Oplismenus***
   Shady places in the Southeast and Texas. (710)

   8. First glume awnless or with an awn shorter than the body of the
   glume .... ***Echinochloa***
   Barnyard grass or jungle rice. Widespread weeds of moist
   places over much of the U.S. (711)

9. Sterile lemmas notched, bearing a delicate awn 1-10 mm long
.... ***Melinis minutiflora* Beauv.**
Molasses grass. Escaped pasture grass of southern Florida. (569)

9. Sterile lemma apex entire, awnless or with a stout awn ... **10**

   10. Plants with underground spikelets .... ***Amphicarpum***
   Peanut grass. Sandy, pine woodlands of the Atlantic
   states. (735)

   10. Underground spikelets absent **11**

11. Fertile lemmas thin and flexible; first glume minute or absent ..
.... **12**

11. Fertile lemmas relatively thick and rigid; first glume present and well-
developed **14**

   12. Panicle about as broad as long at maturity ... ***Digitaria***[57]
   Sandy hills and fields of the eastern, southeastern, and southwestern U.S. (585)

   12. Panicle much broader than long at maturity **13**

13. First glume missing; second glume and fertile lemma densely short-
hairy .... ***Anthaenantia***
Pine woodlands, N. Carolina to Florida and Texas. (569)

13. First glume small, but present; second glume and fertile lemma with
long, silky hairs .... ***Digitaria***
Sourgrass or cottontop. Dry fields and hills of the Southwest. (570)

14. Fertile lemma and palea with tufts of hairs at their tips ...
.... ***Lasiacis divaricata* (L.) Hitchc.**
Tibisee. Borders of wooded areas in southern Florida. (706)

14. Fertile lemma and palea without tufts of hair at their tips .
.... **15**

15. Second glume slightly inflated and sac-like at the base; fertile floret on a short stalk within the spikelet ....
.... ***Sacciolepis striata* (L.) Nash.**
Moist places, southeastern states to Texas and Oklahoma. (708)

15. Second glume not inflated and not sac-like at its base; the fertile floret sessile within the spikelet **16**

16. Floret awned or awn-tipped; tip of palea free from lemma .
.... ***Echinochloa***
Barnyard grass and jungle rice. Widespread weeds of moist places over much of the U.S. (711)

16. Floret awnless; tip of palea enclosed by the lemma ....
.... ***Panicum***[58]
Panic grasses. H & C recognized almost 200 species in this very diverse group of grasses occurring throughout the U.S. (626)

NOTES

1. As treated here, *Arundinaria gigantea* includes *A. tecta.*
2. Throughout this key, the number in parentheses at the end of a statement is the page number of that plant in Hitchcock, A.S. 1950. Manual of the grasses of the United States. U.S.D.A. Misc. Publ. No. 200. I will refer to this book as "H & C" in the remaining notes.
3. This grass is not included in H & C.
4. This grass is called *Phragmites communis* in H & C.
5. The names of species used in H & C have been changed.
6. As treated here, *Zea* includes the genus *Euchlaena.*
7. This grass is called *Distichlis texana* in H & C.
8. As treated here, the genus includes *Heleochloa.*
9. This genus was treated as part of *Tridens* in H & C.
10. The generic name is spelled *Munroa* in H & C and most other recent floras.
11. These species belong to the section *Chondrosium* of *Bouteloua.*
12. As treated here, *Setaria* includes species once assigned to *Panicum* subgenus *Paurochaetium.*
13. *Aegilops* is sometimes merged with *Triticum.*
14. This genus is spelled *Elyonurus* in H & C.
15. This grass was included in *Manisuris* in H & C.
16. This genus was referred to *Manisuris* in H & C.
17. This genus was treated as part of *Andropogon* in H & C.
18. This genus was treated as part of *Elymus* in H & C.
19. This species is also placed in the genus *Neeragrostis* by some recent workers.
20. As treated here, *Tridens* is a more narrowly defined genus than it appears in H & C because several species are now referred to *Erioneuron.*
21. These grasses have been assigned to *Pleuropogon* by most recent American authors.
22. This plant was referred to the genus *Ectosperma* in H & C.
23. These species were referred to *Festuca* in H & C.
24. This grass was referred to *Agropyron* in H & C.
25. Although grasses of the genus *Elymus* typically have two to several spikelets per node, some have only one. These are often difficult to distinguish from *Agropyron.* May I suggest that if you have a coin in your pocket, you may find it useful at this point.
26. *Andropogon* is treated here in the narrow sense. Other species traditionally assigned to this genus are now placed in *Bothriochloa* and *Schizachyrium.*
27. *Bothriochloa* was treated as *Andropogon* section *Amphilophis* in H & C.
28. You have keyed the staminate plants of a dioecious species.
29. As treated here, *Digitaria* includes *Trichachne* and *Leptoloma,* both recognized as distinct genera in H & C.
30. These plants belong to the section *Atheropogon* of *Bouteloua.*
31. *Paspalidium* was treated as *Panicum,* group "*Geminata*" by H & C.
32. As treated here, *Chloris* is restricted to the section *Euchloris* of H & C.
33. *Eustachys* was treated as a section of *Chloris* by H & C.
34. *Diplachne* was not considered distinct from *Leptochloa* by H & C.
35. *Leptochloa,* as treated here in the narrow sense, is distinct from *Diplachne.*
36. *Vulpia* was treated as a section of *Festuca* in H & C.

37. This grass was referred to the genus *Scleropoa* by H & C.
38. This plant was called *Leptoloma cognatum* by H & C.
39. This plant was called *Rhynchelytrum roseum* by H & C.
40. A few species, as in the Californian *Elymus condensatus*, have compound spikes.
41. These species were treated as belonging in *Trichachne* by H & C.
42. This is the proliferated form of plants belonging to the species.
43. This grass was referred to *Hesperochloa* in H & C.
44. The genus is treated here in the narrow sense. *Distichlis texana* has been transferred to *Allolepis* and the two remaining species of H & C have been merged.
45. As treated here, several species listed for *Tridens* in H & C have been transferred to *Erioneuron*.
46. The plants that key here belong to only certain sections of *Bromus*.
47. As treated here, *Deschampsia* does not include *D. atropurpurea*, which has been transferred to *Vahlodea*.
48. This species was assigned to *Deschampsia* in H & C.
49. As treated here, *Festuca* does not include the annual species that have now been assigned to the genus *Vulpia*.
50. Other species traditionally assigned to *Uniola* have been transferred to the genus *Chasmanthium*.
51. These grasses were assigned to *Uniola* in H & C.
52. As treated here, the genus includes grasses sometimes assigned to the genus *Torreyochloa*.
53. Some species assigned to *Glyceria* by H & C have since been transferred to *Puccinellia*.
54. This species was referred to *Scleropoa* by H & C.
55. A few species that key here were assigned to *Panicum* subgenus *Paurochaetium* by H & C.
56. Some species of *Cenchrus* have been assigned to *Pennisetum*, especially those with bristly, rather than spiny, involucres.
57. As treated here, *Digitaria* includes species assigned to *Leptoloma* and *Trichachne* by H & C.
58. As treated here, *Panicum* excludes the subgenus *Paurochaetium,* but includes the subgenera *Panicum* (called *Eupanicum* in H & C) and *Dichanthelium*.

64

EXCLUDED GENERA

X *Agroelymus*
An intergeneric hybrid involving *Agropyron* and *Elymus**

X *Agrohordeum*
An intergeneric hybrid involving *Agropyron* and *Hordeum**

X *Agropogon*
An intergeneric hybrid involving *Agrostis* and *Polypogon**

X *Agrositanion*
An intergeneric hybrid involving *Agropyron* and *Sitanion**

Ampelodesmos
No longer persisting in the U.S. outside cultivation

Aneurolepidium
Not treated as distinct from *Elymus*

Asperella
Not treated as distinct from *Hystrix*

Avenochloa
Not treated as distinct from *Helictotrichon*

Bromopsis
Not treated as distinct from *Bromus*

Ceratochloa
Not treated as distinct from *Bromus*

Chaetotropis
Not treated as distinct from *Polypogon*

Clinelymus
Not treated as distinct from *Elymus*

Dichanthelium
Not treated as distinct from *Panicum*

Dissanthelium
Presumably extinct in the United States

X *Elyhordeum*
An intergeneric hybrid involving *Elymus* and *Hordeum**

X *Elysitanion*
An intergeneric hybrid involving *Elymus* and *Sitanion**

Euchlaena
Not treated as distinct from *Zea*

Heleochloa
Not treated as distinct from *Crypsis*

Hesperochloa
Not treated as distinct from *Leucopoa*

Leptoloma
 Not treated as distinct from *Digitaria*

Leymus
 Not treated as distinct from *Elymus*

Manisuris
 Our species have been assigned to *Coelorachis* and *Hemarthria.*

Neeragrostis
 Not treated as distinct from *Eragrostis*

Olyra
 Presumably extinct in the United States

Phanopyrum
 Not treated as distinct from *Panicum*

Pharus
 Presumably extinct in the United States

Podagrostis
 Not treated as distinct from *Agrostis*

Psathyrostachys
 Not treated as distinct from *Elymus*

Ptilagrostis
 Not treated as distinct from *Stipa*

Scleropoa
 Not treated as distinct from *Catapodium*

X *Sitordeum*
 An intergeneric hybrid involving *Sitanion* and *Hordeum**

Steinchisma
 Not treated as distinct from *Panicum*

X *Stiporyzopsis*
 An intergeneric hybrid involving *Stipa* and *Oryzopsis**

Terrellia
 Not treated as distinct from *Elymus*

Thysanolaena
 Not persisting outside of cultivation

Torreyochloa
 Not treated as distinct from *Puccinellia*

Trichachne
 Not treated as distinct from *Digitaria*

Trichloris
 Not treated as distinct from *Chloris*

---

*Although I am not comfortable in rejecting generic names applied to intergeneric hybrids, their acceptance may be even less satisfactory. Hybridization is common in the grasses and this practice of providing formal taxonomic status to its products could become unwieldy.

USEFUL LITERATURE
FOR THE IDENTIFICATION OF GRASSES

PART A: GENERAL TREATMENTS OF GRASSES (WORLD-WIDE AND U.S.)

Beal, W.J. 1887-1896. The grasses of North America. 2 vols. Henry Holt and Co. New York. 457 pp. and 706 pp.

Bews, J.W. 1929. The world's grasses, their differentiation, distribution, economics and ecology. Longman, Green and Co. London. 408 pp.

Brown, L. 1979. Grasses, an identification guide. Peterson Nature Library. Houghton Mifflin Co. 240 pp.

Gould, F.W. 1951. Grasses of the southwestern United States. Univ. of Arizona Biol. Sci. Bull. No. 7, 22(1): 1-343.

Hackel, E. 1890. The true grasses. Translated from Die Natürlichen Pflanzenfamilien by F. Lamson-Scribner and E.A. Southworth. Henry Holt and Co. New York. 228 pp.

Hanson, A.A. 1965. Grass varieties in the United States. Revised. U.S.D.A. Agric. Handbook No. 170. 102 pp.

Hitchcock, A.S. 1931. Poaceae. North American Flora 17(4): 289-354.

Hitchcock, A.S. 1935. Poaceae. North American Flora 17(5): 355-418; 17(6):419-482.

Hitchcock,· A.S. 1936. The genera of grasses of the United States. Revised. U.S.D.A. Bull. 772:1-302.

Hitchcock, A.S. 1937. Poaceae. North American Flora 17(7):483-542.

Hitchcock, A.S., J.R. Swallen, and A. Chase. 1939. Poaceae. North American Flora 17(8):543-638.

Hitchcock, A.S. 1951. Manual of the grasses of the United States. Second edition revised by Agnes Chase. Misc. Publ. No. 200. U.S. Dept. of Agriculture. Washington, D.C. 1051 pp.

Knobel, E. 1980. Field guide to the grasses, sedges and rushes of the United States. Second revised edition by M.E. Faust. Dover Publ. New York. 83 pp.

Lamson-Scribner, F. 1900. American grasses. Third edition. U.S.D.A. Div. Agrost. Bull. 7:1-319.

Lamson-Scribner, F. 1900. American grasses. III. Second edition. U.S.D.A. Div. Agrost. Bull. 20:1-197.

Lamson-Scribner, F. 1901. American grasses. II. Second edition. U.S.D.A. Div. Agrost. Bull. 17:1-349.

Leithead, H.L. et al. 1971. 100 Native forage grasses in 11 southern states. Agric. Handbook No. 389. U.S.D.A. Washington, D.C. 216 pp.

Nash, G.V. 1909. Poaceae. North American Flora 17(1):77-98.

Nash, G.V. 1912. Poaceae. North American Flora 17(2):99-196.

Nash, G.V. and A.S. Hitchcock. 1915. Poaceae. North American Flora 17(3):197-288.

Phillips, C.E. 1962. Some grasses of the Northeast; a key to their identification by vegetative characters. Univ. Delaware Agric. Exp. Stat. Field Manual No. 2. 77 pp.

Pilger, R. 1956. Gramineae II. In, Die Natürlichen Pflanzenfamilien, Melchoir H. and E. Werdermann (Editors). Band 14d. Duncker and Humblot. Berlin. 225 pp.

Pilger, R. 1960. Gramineae III. In, Die Natürlichen Pflanzenfamilien, H. Harms and J. Mattfeld (Editors). Band 14e. Duncker and Humblot. Berlin. 208 pp.

Pohl, R.W. 1978. How to know the grasses. 3rd edition. W.C. Brown Co. Dubuque, Iowa. 200 pp.

Potztal, E. 1956. Gramineae III. In, Die Natürlichen Pflanzenfamilien, Melchoir H. and E. Werdermann (Editors). Band 14e. Duncker and Humblot. Berlin.

Rydberg, P.A. and C.L. Shear. 1897. A report upon the grasses and forage plants of the Rocky Mountain region. U.S.D.A. Div. Agrost. Bull. 5:1-48.

Vasey, G. 1883. The grasses of the United States: being a synopsis of the tribes and genera, with descriptions of the genera and a list of species. Dept. of Agric. Special Report No. 63. 47 pp.

Vasey, G. 1887. Grasses of the South. U.S.D.A. Bot. Div. Bull. 3:1-63.

Vasey, G. 1890-1891. Grasses of the Southwest. Parts I and II. U.S.D.A. Div. Bot. Bull. No. 12.

Vasey, G. 1892. Monograph of the grasses of the United States and British America. Part I. Contr. U.S. Natl. Herb. 3:1-89.

Vasey, G. 1892-1893. Grasses of the Pacific Slope, including Alaska and adjacent islands. Parts I and II. U.S.D.A. Div. Bot. Bull. No. 13.

Weintraub, F.C. 1953. Grasses introduced into the United States. U.S. D.A. Agric. Handbook No. 58. 79 pp.

Young, R.A. and J.R. Haun. 1961. Bamboo in the United States: description, culture, and utilization. Key to genera by F.A. McClure. U.S.D.A. Agric. Handbook No. 193. 74 pp.

PART B: TREATMENTS OF GRASSES AT THE STATE LEVEL

Alabama:

Banks, D.J. 1965. A checklist of the grasses (Gramineae) of Alabama. Castanea 30:84-96.

Mell, P.H. 1889. Grasses of Alabama and their cultivation. Alabama Exp. Stat. Bull. No. 6:1-35.

Arizona:

Copple, R.F. and C.P. Pase. 1978. A vegetative key to some common Arizona range grasses. Gen. Tech. Rep. RM-53. 106 pp.

Humphrey, R.R. 1970. Arizona range grasses. Univ. Arizona Press. Tucson. 159 pp.

See also:

Kearney, T.H. and R.H. Peebles. 1960. Arizona flora. Univ. of California Press. Berkeley. 1085 pp.

Arkansas:

Moore, D.M. 1961. Revised and annotated catalogue of the grasses of Arkansas. Arkansas Acad. Sci. Proc. 15:9-25.

Robinson, A., Jr. 1964. Report on the Gramineae of the Arkansas Salem Plateau. Trans. Kansas Acad. Sci. 67:460-469.

California:

Beetle, A.A. 1947. Distribution of the native grasses of California. Hilgardia 17:309-357.

Crampton, B. 1974. Grasses in California. University of California Press. Berkeley. 178 pp.

Sampson, A.W. and A. Chase. 1927. Range grasses of California. Univ. Calif. Agric. Exp. Stat. Bull. 430:1-94.

See also:

Munz, P.A. 1959. A California flora. In collaboration with D. Keck. Univ. of California Press. Berkeley. 1681 pp.

Munz, P.A. 1968. Supplement to a California flora. Univ. of Calif. Press. Berkeley. 224 pp.

Munz, P.A. 1974. A flora of Southern California. Univ. of California Press. Berkeley. 1086 pp.

Colorado:

Harrington, H.D. 1946. Grasses of Colorado. Colorado A. & M. College. Ft. Collins. 167 pp.

Harrington, H.D. and L.W. Durrell. 1944. Key to some Colorado grasses in vegetative condition. Colorado Agric. Exp. Stat. Tech. Bull. 33:1-86.

See also:

Harrington, H.D. 1954. Manual of the plants of Colorado. Swallow Press. Denver. 666 pp.

Florida:

Hall, D.W. 1978. The grasses of Florida. Ph. D. dissertation. Univ. of Florida. University Microfilms International. Ann Arbor. 498 pp.

See also:

Long, R.W. and O. Lakela. 1971. A flora of tropical Florida. Univ. of Miami Press. Coral Gables. 962 pp.

Ward. D.B. 1968. Checklist of the vascular flora of Florida. Part 1. Tech. Bull. 726, Agric. Exp. Stations. Univ. of Fla. Gainsville. 72 pp.

Georgia:

Use:

Duncan, W.H. and J.T. Kartesz. 1980. Vascular flora of Georgia. An annotated checklist. Univ. Georgia Press. Athens. 158 pp.

Idaho:

Use:

Davis, R.J. 1952. Flora of Idaho. W.C. Brown Co. Dubuque. 828 pp.

Illinois:

Glassman, S.F. 1964. Grass flora of the Chicago region. Amer. Midl. Nat. 72:1-49.

Mohlenbrock. R.H. 1972. The illustrated flora of Illinois: Grasses: *Bromus* to *Papsalum.* Southern Illinois Univ. Press. Carbondale. 332 pp.

Mohlenbrock. R.H. 1973. The illustrated flora of Illinois: Grasses: *Panicum* to *Danthonia.* Southern Illinois University Press. Carbondale. 378 pp.

Mosher, E. 1918. The grasses of Illinois. Univ. Ill. Agric. Exp. Stat. Bull. 205:261-425.

Indiana:

Deam, C.C. 1929. Grasses of Indiana. W.B. Burford. Indianapolis. 356 pp.

Troop, J. 1889. Grasses of Indiana. Indiana Exp. Stat. Bull. 29:1-42.

See also:

Deam, C.C. 1940. Flora of Indiana. Dept. of Conservation. Indianapolis. 1236 pp.

Iowa:

Pammel, L.H. 1901. Grasses of Iowa. Part I. Iowa Exp. Stat. Bull. 54: 71-344.

Pammel, L.H. 1904. Grasses of Iowa. Part II. Suppl. Report Ia. Geological Survey 1903. 436 pp.

Pohl, R.W. 1966. The grasses of Iowa. Iowa State J. of Sci. 40(4):341-566.

Kansas:

Gates, F.C. 1937. Grasses in Kansas. Report of the Kansas State Board of Agric. 55(220-A):1-349.

Hitchcock, A.S. 1896. The grasses of Kansas. Trans. Kansas Acad. Sci. 14: 135-149.

Hitchcock, A.S. and G.L. Clothier. 1899. Native agricultural grasses of Kansas. Kansas Exp. Stat. Bull. 87:1-29.

See also:

Barkley, T.H. 1968. A manual of the flowering plants of Kansas. Kansas State Univ. Endowment Assoc. Manhattan. 402 pp.

McGregor, R.L., R.E. Brooks, and L.A. Hauser. 1976. Checklist of Kansas vascular plants. Tech. Publ. State Biol. Surv. Kansas 2:1-168. .

Kentucky:

Garman, H. 1900. Kentucky forage plants—the grasses. Kentucky Exp. Stat. Bull. 87:55-122.

See also:

Braun, E.L. 1943. An annotated catalog of spermatophytes of Kentucky. Publ. by the author. Cincinnati, Ohio. 161 pp.

Louisiana:

Allen, C.M. 1980. Grasses of Louisiana. Univ. of Southwestern Louisiana. Lafayette. 358 pp.

Maine:

Use:

Ogden, E.C., F.H. Steinmetz, and F. Hyland. 1948. Checklist of the vascular plants of Maine. Bull. Joss. Bot. Soc. 8:1-70.

Maryland:

Norton, J.B.S. 1931. Maryland grasses. Maryland Agric. Exp. Stat. Bull. 323:251-326.

Massachusetts:

Use:

Ahmadjian, V. 1979. Flowering plants of Massachusetts. Univ. of Mass. Press. Amherst. 582 pp.

Michigan:

Moore, W.O. 1977. Some very common grasses. Michigan Bot. 16(4):167-188.

See also:

Voss, E.G. 1972. Michigan flora: A guide to the identification and occurrence of the native and naturalized seed-plants of the state. Part I: Gymnosperms and monocots. Cranbrook Inst. Sci. Bull. 55. 488 pp.

Minnesota:

Use:

Moore, J.W. and R.M. Tryon, Jr. 1946. A preliminary checklist of the flowering plants, ferns, and fern allies of Minnesota. Univ. of Minnesota Press. Minneapolis. 99 pp.

Mississippi:

Bennett, H.W., R.O. Hammons, and W.R. Weissinger. 1950. The identification of 76 grasses by vegetative morphology. Miss. State College Agric. Exp. Stat. Tech. Bull. 31:1-108.

See also:

Lowe, E.N. 1921. Plants of Mississippi. Bull. Mississippi State Geol. Survey 17:1-292.

Missouri:

Kucera, C.L. 1961. The grasses of Missouri. Univ. of Missouri Press. Columbia. 241 pp.

See also:

Steyermark, J.A. 1963. Flora of Missouri. Iowa State Univ. Press. Ames. 1725 pp.

Montana:

Hitchcock, C.L. 1936. A key to the grasses of Montana based upon vegetative characters. J.S. Swift Co. St. Louis. 28 pp.

See also:

Booth, W.E. 1950. Flora of Montana (Part I, conifers and monocots). Montana State College Research Foundation. Bozeman. 232 pp.

Nebraska:

Bates, J.M. 1892. The grasses of north-western Nebraska. Report Nebraska State Board of Agric. 1891:130-134.

Bessey, C.E. 1892. A preliminary list of the grasses of Nebraska. Report Nebraska State Board Agric. 1891:124-130.

Bessey, C.E. 1893. A preliminary description of the native and introduced grasses of Nebraska. Report Nebraska State Board Agric. 1892:209-279.

Bessey, C.E. 1905. The grasses of Nebraska. Annual Report State Board Agric. 1904:175-205.

Frolik, A.L. and F.D. Keim. 1938. Common native grasses of Nebraska. Univ. Nebraska Exp. Stat. Circular 59. 52 pp.

Keim, F.D., G.W. Beadle, and A.L. Frolik. 1932. The identification of the more important prairie hay grasses of Nebraska by their vegetative characters. Univ. Nebraska Agric. Exp. Stat. Res. Bull. 65:1-40.

Rydberg, P.A. 1894. The grasses of central Nebraska. Report Nebraska State Board Agric. 1893:69-73.

Smith, J.G. 1893. The grasses of the Sand Hills of northern Nebraska. Report Nebraska State Board Agric. 1892:280-291.

Wilcox, E.M., G.K.K. Link, and V.W. Pool. 1915. A handbook of Nebraska grasses. Nebraska Agric. Exp. Stat. Bull. 148:1-120.

See also:

Petersen, N.F. 1923. Flora of Nebraska; ferns, conifers and flowering plants of the state, with keys for their identification. Third edition. Publ. by the author. Lincoln. 220 pp.

Nevada:

Swallen, J.R. 1940. Gramineae of Nevada. Contr. Toward a Flora of Nevada. No. 1. 91 pp.

New Hampshire:

Hodgdon, A.R., G.E. Crow, and F.L. Steele. 1979. Grasses of New Hampshire. I. Tribes Poeae (Festuceae) and Triticeae (Hordeae). Station Bulletin 512. New Hampshire Agric. Exp. Sta. Durham. 53 pp.

See also:

Pease, A.S. 1964. A flora of Northern New Hampshire. New England Bot. Club. Cambridge. 278 pp.

New Jersey:

Use:

Stone, W. 1973. The plants of southern New Jersey. Quarterman. Boston. pp. 25-828.

New Mexico:

Wooten, E.O. and P.C. Standley. 1912. The grasses and grass-like plants of New Mexico. New Mexico Exp. Stat. Bull. 81:3-176.

See also:

Martin, W.C. and C.R. Hutchins. 1980. A flora of New Mexico. 2 vols. J. Cramer. 2591 pp.

New York:

Smith, S.J. 1965. Checklist of the grasses of New York state. New York State Museum and Science Service Bull. No. 403. 44 pp.

North Carolina:

Blomquist, H.L. 1948. The grasses of North Carolina. Duke Univ. Press. Durham, North Carolina. 276 pp.

See also:

Radford, A.E., H.E. Ahles, and C.R. Bell. 1968. Manual of the vascular flora of the Carolinas. Univ. of North Carolina Press. Chapel Hill. 1183 pp.

North Dakota:

Williams, T.A. 1897. Grasses and forage plants of the Dakotas. U.S.D.A. Div. Agrost. Bull. 6:1-47.

See also:

Stevens, O.A. 1963. Handbook of North Dakota plants. North Dakota Inst. for Regional Stud. Fargo. 324 pp.

Ohio:

Schaffner, J.H. 1917. The grasses of Ohio. Ohio Biol. Surv. Bull. 2(5): 255-329.

See also:

Braun, E.L. 1967. The vascular flora of Ohio. Vol. 1. The Monocotyledoneae. Ohio State Univ. Press. Columbus. 464 pp.

Weishaupt, C.G. 1971. Vascular plants of Ohio; a manual for use in field and laboratory. 3rd ed. Kendall/Hunt Publ. Dubuque. 292 pp.

Oklahoma:

Featherly, H.I. 1946. Manual of grasses of Oklahoma. Okla. State Univ. Bull. 43(21):1-137.

See also:

Waterfall, U.T. 1972. Keys to the flora of Oklahoma. 5th ed. Published by the author. Student Union Bookstore. Oklahoma State University. Stillwater. 246 pp.

Oregon:

Use:

Peck, M.E. 1961. A manual of the higher plants of Oregon. 2nd ed. Oregon State Univ. Press. Corvallis. 936 pp.

Pennsylvania:

Gress, E. M. 1924. The grasses of Pennsylvania. Bull. Penn. Dept. Agric. 384(7):1-245.

Pohl. R.W. 1947. A taxonomic study on the grasses of Pennsylvania. Amer. Midl. Nat. 38(3):513-604.

Rhode Island:

Use:

Palmatier, E.A. 1952. Flora of Rhode Island. Univ. of Rhode Island. Kingston. 75 pp.

South Carolina:

Use:

Radford, A.E., H.E. Ahles, and C.R. Bell. 1968. Manual of the vascular flora of the Carolinas. Univ. of North Carolina Press. Chapel Hill. 1183 pp.

South Dakota:

Van Bruggen, T. n.d. A key for the identification of grasses of South Dakota. Mimeographed. Botany Department. Univ. S. Dakota. 27 pp.

Williams, T.A. 1897. Grasses and forage plants of the Dakotas. U.S.D.A. Div. Agrost. Bull. 6:1-47.

See also:

Van Bruggen, T. 1976. Vascular plants of South Dakota. Iowa State University Press. Ames. 538 pp.

74

Tennessee:

Killebrew, J.B. 1878. The grasses of Tennessee; including cereals, and forage plants. The American Co. Nashville. 511 pp.

Lamson-Scribner, F. 1892-1894. The grasses of Tennessee. Bull. Agric. Exp. Stat. Univ. Tenn. Part I. 5(2):27-119. Part II. 7(1):1-141.

Texas:

Gould, F.W. 1975. The grasses of Texas. Texas A & M Univ. Press. College Station. 653 pp.

Gould, F.W. 1978. Common Texas grasses. Texas A & M Univ. Press. College Station. 267 pp.

Gould, F.W. & T.W. Box. 1965. Grasses of the Texas coastal bend. Texas A & M Univ. Press. College Station. 186 pp.

Silveus, W.A. 1933. Texas grasses. Publ. by the author. San Antonio. 782 pp.

Tharp, B.J. 1952. Texas range grasses. Univ. Texas Press. Austin. 125 pp.

Utah:

Flowers, S. 1959. Common grasses of Utah. 3rd ed. Univ. of Utah Press. Salt Lake City. 122 pp.

Harrison, B.F. 1939. An annotated list of Utah grasses. Proc. Utah Acad. Sci. 16:23-35.

Parker, K.G., L.R. Mason, and J.F. Valentine. 1979. Utah grasses. Extension Circular 384. Cooperative Extension Service, Utah State Univ. 69 pp.

See also:

Welsh, S.L. and G. Moore. 1973. Utah plants: Tracheophyta. 3rd ed. Brigham Young Univ. Press. Provo. 474 pp.

Vermont:

Use:

Seymour, F.C. 1969. The flora of Vermont. 4th edition. Agric. Exp. Sta. Bull. 660. Univ. of Vermont. Burlington. 393 pp.

Virginia:

Use:

Massey, A.B. 1961. Virginia flora. Virginia Agric. Exp. Sta. Tech. Bull. 152. Blacksburg. 258 pp.

West Virginia:

Core, E.L., E.E. Berkley, and H.A. Davis. 1944. West Virginia grasses. West Virginia Agric. Exp. Stat. Bull. 313. 96 pp.

See also:

Strausbaugh, P.D. and E.L. Core. 1978. Flora of West Virginia. Second Edition. Seneca Books. Grantsville, West Virginia. 1120 pp.

Wisconsin:

Fassett, N.C. 1951. Grasses of Wisconsin. Univ. of Wisconsin Press. Madison. 173 pp.

Freckmann, R.W. 1972. Grasses of central Wisconsin. Reports on the Fauna and Flora of Wisconsin. Report No. 6. Mus. of Nat. Hist. Univ. of Wisconsin. Stevens Point. 81 pp.

Wyoming:

Beetle, A.A. & M. May. 1971. Grasses of Wyoming. Res. J. 39. Agric. Exp. Sta. Univ. of Wyoming. Laramie. 151 pp.

Porter, C.L. 1964. Poaceae (Gramineae). A flora of Wyoming. Part 3. Univ. Wyoming Agric. Exp. Stat. Bull. 418. 80 pp.

See also:

Dorn, R.D. 1977. Manual of the vascular plants of Wyoming. Garland Publ. Co. New York. 1498 pp.

PART C: GENERAL AND REGIONAL FLORAS THAT INCLUDE GRASSES

Abrams, L. 1955. An illustrated flora of the Pacific states. Vol. I. Stanford University Press. Stanford. 538 pp.

Barkley, T. (Editor). 1977. Atlas of the flora of the Great Plains. Iowa State Univ. Press. Ames. 600 pp.

Cronquist, A. et al. 1977. Intermountain flora. Vol. 6. Columbia University Press. New York. 584 pp.

Fernald, M.L. 1950. Gray's manual of botany. 8th ed. American Book Co. New York. 1632 pp.

Gilkey, H.M. and L.R. Dennis. 1980. Handbook of northwestern plants. Oregon State University Bookstores. Corvallis. 507 pp.

Gleason, H.A. 1963. New Britton and Brown illustrated flora of the northeastern United States and adjacent Canada. Vol. I. Hafner Publ. Co. New York. 482 pp.

Gleason, H.A. & A.C. Cronquist. 1963. Manual of the vascular plants of the northeastern United States and adjacent Canada. Van Nostrand Co. Princeton, N.J. 810 pp.

Hitchcock, C.L. & A. Cronquist. 1973. Flora of the Pacific Northwest: an illustrated manual. University of Washington Press. Seattle. 730 pp.

Hitchcock, C.L. et al. 1969. Vascular plants of the Pacific Northwest. Vol. I. University of Washington Press. Seattle. 914 pp.

Rydberg, P.A. 1922. Flora of the Rocky Mountains and adjacent plains. Reprinted in 1954, Hafner Publ. Co. New York. 1143 pp.

Rydberg, P.A. 1932. Flora of the prairies and plains of central North America. Reprinted (1971) by Dover Publ. Co. New York. 2 vols. 969 pp.

Seymour, F.C. 1969. Flora of New England. C.E. Tuttle. Rutland, Vermont. 596 pp.

Small, J.K. 1933. Manual of the southeastern flora. Univ. of North Carolina Press. Chapel Hill. 1554 pp.

Weber, W.A. 1976. Rocky Mountain flora. 5th edition. Colorado Associated Univ. Press. Boulder. 479 pp.

GLOSSARY

achene A dry, single-seeded fruit whose seed coat and fruit wall are separate from one another.

acute Sharp-pointed.

androecium The male part of a flower, consisting of stamens.

annual Living for a single growing season.

anther The sac-like, pollen-producing part of a stamen.

appressed Lying against a surface or, in the case of inflorescence branches, against a central or principal axis.

attenuate Gradually narrowed to a slender point.

auricles The paired, ear-shaped appendages at the apex of the sheath in some grasses.

axillary inflorescence An inflorescence which arises from a side or lateral position on a culm.

balanced Having spikelets more or less equally inserted on both sides of a rachis.

basifixed Said of an anther that is attached at its base to the filament, as opposed to its midpoint.

beautiful Of or pertaining to grasses, especially native species.

bifid Two-cleft or two-lobed, as in the apex of a lemma or glume.

blade The flattened, expanded portion of a leaf.

body The portion of a glume, lemma, or palea exclusive of an awn.

bract A reduced leaf.

bristle A short, stiff hair.

bulb A subterranean plant structure consisting of a series of overlapping leaf bases inserted on a much-reduced stem axis.

bulblet A small bulb.

callus The hardened, often pointed base of a lemma or floret.

capillary Hair-like.

capitate Aggregated into a dense, head-like cluster.

caryopsis A dry, single-seeded fruit whose seed coat and fruit wall are fused together; the fruit of the grass family.

ciliate Fringed with marginal hairs.

closed sheath A sheath in which the two edges are fused with one another to form a continuous cylinder around the culm.

compound raceme An inflorescence type in which the peduncle bears two or more branches, each bearing a raceme of spikelets.

compound rame An inflorescence type in which the peduncle bears two or more branches, each bearing a rame of spikelets.

compound spike An inflorescence type in which the peduncle bears two or more branches, each bearing a spike of spikelets.

compressed Flattened.

cordate Heart-shaped.

corm A dense, vertical, subterranean stem surrounded by dry, papery leaf bases.

culm. The stem of a grass plant.

digitate Having components that radiate from a central point, as in fingers of a hand.

dioecious A species in which staminate and pistillate spikelets occur on separate plants, as in buffalo grass.

disarticulation The separation or disjoining of spikelet parts or of rachis sections from one another.

distichous Inserted in two vertical rows, as in leaves on a culm or bracts on a rachilla.

divergent Spread apart from one another, as in inflorescence branches.

dorsally compressed Flattened as if pressure had been brought to bear on the back of a bract, as opposed to the sides of the bract.

elliptical In the form of a flattened circle.

entire A margin without teeth or lobes.

exserted Protruding beyond or out of, as in an inflorescence from a sheath.

fascicle A tight cluster or clump, as in leaves, axillary culms, or spikelets.

filament The delicate stalk that supports an anther.

floret A subunit of a spikelet, consisting of a lemma, palea, and flower.

geniculate Sharply-bent, as in a culm or awn.

glabrous Without hairs.

glume Either of the two sterile bracts at the base of the grass spikelet.

grain The semitechnical term for the fruit of the grass family; the caryopsis.

gynoecium The female part of the flower, consisting of the seed-producing components.

H & C An abbreviation for Hitchcock and Chase, authors of the *Manual of the Grasses of the United States.*

herbaceous Having the features of an herb.

hirsute With coarse, more or less erect hairs.

indurate Hard, as in texture.

inflorescence The flowering portion of a grass plant; the arrangement of spikelets on a culm.

internode The region between two consecutive nodes on a culm.

involucre An organized set of bracts or branchlets that surrounds a spikelet or floret or that forms a series or set beneath it.

keel A prominent ridge or rib, as in the longitudinal feature found on some glumes, lemmas, and paleas.

lanceolate Said of a leaf blade or bract that is narrow and which tapers on both ends and which is widest above the middle.

laterally compressed Flattened, as if pressure were brought to bear on the sides of a bract, as opposed to the back of the bract.

lemma One of two bracts of a floret, the other being the palea, which enclose the flower.

ligule The membranous flap or projection (or series of hairs) at the junction of the sheath and blade of a grass leaf.

lodicule The microscopic perianth remnants in the grass flower.

monoecious A species in which staminate and pistillate spikelets or florets occur on the same plant.

mucro A short, sharp point or extension, as seen at the apex of a bract.

mucronate Bearing a mucro or short, sharp point or extension.

nerve A strand of vascular tissue, seen as ridges on the surface of glumes, lemmas, and paleas.

neuter Lacking reproductive structures; sterile.

node The point or region on a culm where a leaf is borne.

oblong Much longer than broad, the sides more or less parallel.

obtuse Blunt in form; also, dull in perception or intellect, as in people who find grasses ugly and boring.

open sheath A sheath in which the two edges touch one another or overlap, but do not fuse to form a continuous cylinder.

ovary The seed-bearing portion of the flower.

ovate Egg-shaped.

palea One of two bracts of a floret, the other being the lemma, which enclose the flower.

panicle An elongate or rounded, much-branched inflorescence in which the spikelets are inserted on ultimate branchlets.

pedicel The stalk that supports a spikelet.

pedicellate Borne on a stalk or pedicel.

peduncle The stalk that supports an entire inflorescence of spikelets.

perennial Living through the years.

perfect A flower, floret, or spikelet which bears both an androecium and a gynoecium.

petiole The stalk that supports a leaf blade.

pistillate A flower, floret, spikelet, or plant which bears only a gynoecium.

plumose Feather-like, as in an awn with fine hairs.

pubescent Hairy, especially short, soft hairs.

raceme An elongate inflorescence in which spikelets with well-developed pedicels are borne on an unbranched central axis, the rachis.

racemose Resembling a raceme in general appearance.

rachilla The unbranched central axis of a spikelet.

rachis The unbranched central axis of a spike, raceme, or rame; the primary axis of a panicle.

rame An elongate inflorescence in which pedicellate and sessile spikelets are borne in repeating pairs or trios along an axis; less frequently, the spikelets are equally or unequally pedicellate.

rank A vertical row, as of leaves on a stem when viewed from above.

rhizomatous Of or pertaining to rhizomes.

rhizome A subterranean, horizontal stem that bears reduced, scaly leaves.

rudiment A small, very poorly developed floret.

scabrous Covered with short, stiff hairs, so as to be rough to the touch.

sessile Seated or attached directly; not stalked.

sheath The lower portion of the grass leaf that surrounds the culm.

spathulate Having a large bract which subtends and often partially surrounds an inflorescence.

spike An elongate inflorescence in which sessile spikelets are borne directly on an unbranched central axis.

spikelet The basic unit of the grass inflorescence, consisting of two glumes and one or more florets.

stamen The pollen-producing organ of a flower, consisting of an anther and a filament.

staminate A flower, floret, spikelet, or plant which bears only an androecium.

sterile Lacking reproductive parts.

sterile lemma A lemma which does not subtend a flower; a remnant of a reduced floret.

stigma The region of the gynoecium that is receptive to pollen; in grasses, the paired, terminal, feathery structures that sit atop the ovary.

stipitate Stalked.

stolon An aerial, horizontal stem, often rooting at the nodes, which bears ordinary foliage leaves.

stoloniferous Of or pertaining to stolons.

subglobose Almost spherical, as in the shape of a floret or grain.

subtend To be below in point of attachment.

terete Round.

terminal inflorescence An inflorescence which arises from the uppermost sheath of a culm.

transverse In a cross direction; across the face or surface of a structure.

tufted In bunches or clumps, as in the culms of a grass plant.

versatile Said of an anther which is attached at its midpoint, so that it moves more or less freely on the filament.

winged Having a wing, a membranous lateral expansion of an organ, as in a winged rachis.